PROCRASTIBAKING

PROCRASTIBAKING

100 Recipes for Getting Nothing Done in the Most Delicious Way Possible

Erin Gardner

ATRIA BOOKS

New York · London · Toronto · Sydney · New Delhi

ATRIA
BOOKS

An Imprint of Simon & Schuster, Inc.
1230 Avenue of the Americas
New York, NY 10020

First Atria Books hardcover edition March 2020

ATRIA BOOKS and colophon are trademarks of Simon & Schuster, Inc.

For information about special discounts for bulk purchases, please contact Simon & Schuster Special Sales at 1-866-506-1949 or business@simonandschuster.com.

The Simon & Schuster Speakers Bureau can bring authors to your live event. For more information or to book an event, contact the Simon & Schuster Speakers Bureau at 1-866-248-3049 or visit our website at www.simonspeakers.com.

Interior design by Jessica Nordskog / Stonesong Press

Food photographs by Stacey Cramp Photography

Manufactured in the United States of America

1 3 5 7 9 10 8 6 4 2

Library of Congress Cataloging-in-Publication Data has been applied for.

ISBN 978-1-9821-1774-0
ISBN 978-1-9821-1775-7 (ebook)

TO ViOLET AND MAXWELL.
ALWAYS BE YOURSELF.

CONTENTS

CHAPTER 1: CASE-OF-THE-MONDAY-MORNING TREATS

CHAPTER 2: CAN'T-COME-TO-THE-PHONE-RIGHT-NOW CONFECTIONS

CHAPTER 3: BETTER-LATE-THAN-NEVER BROWNIES AND BARS

CHAPTER 4: COOKIES. MAKE ALL THE COOKIES.

CHAPTER 5: LATE-FOR-EVERYTHING LOAF CAKES

CHAPTER 6: FEAR-OF-SUCCESS SNACK CAKES

CHAPTER 7: THANKS-FOR-YOUR-PATIENCE PIES AND TARTS

CHAPTER 8: SORRY-FOR-THE-DELAYED-RESPONSE SAVORY BAKES

CHAPTER 9: THiS MAY TAKE AWHiLE: PROCRASTi-MASTERPiECES

Co

iNTRODUCTiON

I AM LITERALLY WRITING THIS THE NIGHT BEFORE IT'S DUE. Not the whole book! That would be totally reckless and quite impossible. I could not write and test 100 recipes in one night. I mean, I wouldn't put it past me . . . but do not fear. The rest of this book was written, with care, over a lifetime of avoiding work, responding to emails, cleaning the house, and making "real" food.

This introduction, however, is being written the night before I hit send and float this *Procrastibaking* book off through space to my editor. It would have been inauthentic to write the introduction to a book about procrastibaking at any other time. I am, in fact, a notorious procrastinator. Lucky for you and me (and my publisher), I always seem to produce my best work shortly before breathlessly flopping over the finish line. So, here goes.

PROCRASTI-WHAT?

CHANCES ARE YOU ALREADY KNOW WHAT PROCRASTIBAKING IS, EVEN IF YOU HAVEN'T HEARD THE TERM BEFORE. Procrastibaking is the fine art of getting nothing done in the most delicious way possible. It's taking a mini vacation, in your kitchen, from the demands of modern life. How can you return those emails when there's dough on your hands? It would be counterproductive to handle clean laundry after dipping chocolates all afternoon. And how can you be expected to do taxes during apple season?!? (Of course, I'm an extension filer.)

Why do we procrastibake?

I'm not a doctor, but I am a baker, so I feel half qualified to answer this question!

Sometimes, the stresses of everyday life need to take a back seat. Our brains need a break from work and the endless to-do list. Procrastibaking is an ideal escape, because once you start baking, you can't stop until you see it to completion. You simply can't let those whipped egg whites fall or that melted chocolate harden in the bowl. Abandoning those adorably yummy gingerbread house pieces would just be cruel. And as every baker knows, meringue waits for no one. Procrastibaking is a perfect pocket of time away from having to exert yourself mentally or physically. Plus, the result is delicious and makes everyone happy. Win-win!

The other thing procrastibaking helps you avoid? That tiny little black hole you carry around in your purse or pocket that allows you access to all of human knowledge and every person you've encountered since birth. Like I said, I'm no doctor, but I don't think we're supposed to have that in our faces 24/7. Our hands were made to make things, not tap and scroll.

I don't believe you're actually a procrastibaker. Is this just some clever ruse to write another baking book?

If you don't believe me, you might believe a little news publication called the *New York Times*? Yes, that's right. I was featured in an article in the *New York Times* with my bad habits on display for the whole world to see. I can't say it was the way I'd always imagined landing in the *Times* food section, but hey, at least I wasn't indicted.

As the story goes, Julia Moskin messaged me via Instagram one afternoon saying she was writing an article on procrastibaking and asked if I wanted to be interviewed for the story. She learned of my procrastibaking in the most thoroughly modern way possible, a hashtag. While I was writing my previous book, *Erin Bakes Cake*, I blew off a day of recipe testing to make blueberry scones and a giant doughnut. In a moment of silly pride, I snapped a pic of the delicious distractions and posted it to Instagram. The caption read, "The baking you do when you're supposed to be doing other baking #procrastibaking." While I was not the first to use this hashtag, I very well may have been the first to use it in regard to baking to avoid other baking. For that, I know I'm a bit of an oddity.

I emailed, she called, I said ridiculous things like comparing myself to a professional athlete (everyone needs to warm up!), a nice man came out and took pictures, and there I was. Happy as a clam, publicly outed for my procrastibaking ways.

I realize that it's, perhaps, a bit absurd to procrastibake when the work you're avoiding is . . . other baking. You're probably much more practical. You may bake to avoid:

- DOING TAXES
- FOLDING LAUNDRY
- CLEANING THE HOUSE
- BATHING YOUR CHILDREN
- ANSWERING THE PHONE
- COOKING REAL FOOD
- TAKING THE SAND TOYS OUT OF THE BACK OF THE CAR SINCE IT'S, UM, DECEMBER
- WASHING THE FLOORS
- MOWING THE LAWN
- REPLYING TO TEXTS AND EMAILS
- PICKING UP THAT THING THAT'S KIND OF POKING OUT FROM UNDER THE COUCH, BUT YOU'RE NOT REALLY SURE WHAT IT IS
- AND SO MUCH MORE!

I, on the other hand, bake to avoid other baking (and let's be real, all those other things, too). I'm a former pastry chef and award-winning bakery owner, and my current "day job" involves developing new cake decorating techniques and recipes for blogs, magazines, and my own blog, *Erin Bakes*. I'm known in the cake community for creating decorating ideas with simple things like candy, chocolate, and cookies, without the use of special tools. Believe it or not, this takes a lot of creativity and brainpower. You wouldn't believe how many things have already been done! Probably everything. It's my job to create that new spin. To get the wheels turning and warm up my brain and hands, I bake something fun, easy, and always delicious. Kobe wouldn't go into a game cold, and neither do I.

Enabling Thoughts

I may not be a historian, anthropologist, or psychologist, but I can Google with the best of them.

ENABLING YOU WITH ANTHROPOLOGY

As far as we know today, humans evolved 200,000 to 300,000 years ago. The first screens were invented in the 1920s. That means our ancestors lived for 200,900 years (give or take) just looking around, moving their bodies, and doing things with their hands all day long. I'm sure it was far more complex than that. You know, survival and all. But they weren't sitting in a chair looking at a screen. That's a relatively new thing for us. Those tiny screens in our pockets that control our every move? We lived without them for 200,970 years or so. The world's oldest oven was found in Croatia dating back 6,500 years. Which means we've been baking 6,400 years longer than we've been creating spreadsheets and TPS reports. Don't blame yourself for your procrastibaking ways. You're being called by your ancestors.

ENABLING YOU WITH PSYCHOLOGY

Did you know that procrastination can be a good thing sometimes? *And*, I didn't just make that up! Actual scientists, academics, economists, and researchers spend their precious time studying the subject. Books other than this one have been written about some of the positive effects of procrastination. Of course, there are other books warning of its perils, but let's look past those for a moment, shall we?

- Procrastination helps you prioritize tasks. Your caveman brain knows which ones aren't actually important; that's why it tells you to bake.

- Procrastination, and procrastibaking specifically, helps you be more creative. Looking at your required tasks with fresh eyes will enable you to see them in a new light, possibly coming up with inventive ways to tackle them. It could happen. Really!

- Procrastibaking is actually active procrastinating, the very best kind! Don't knock yourself for building a layer cake instead of doing what you were supposed to do. It's still better than lying on the couch scrolling through socials like a zombie.

ENABLING YOU WITH HISTORY

I swear, I didn't make these up.

- Martin Luther King Jr.'s "I Have A Dream" speech and Abraham Lincoln's Gettysburg Address were both written shortly before they were delivered.

- The Dalai Lama is supposedly a notorious procrastinator. Probably because he knows that space and time are all just an illusion, or something.

- Margaret Atwood has been quoted as saying she doesn't even sit down to start writing until 3 p.m. I would include other famous writers, but I'm pretty sure it applies to all of them.

- Leonardo da Vinci was a notorious doodler, blowing off days earmarked for painting by scribbling away, letting his mind wander, and inventing little things like the helicopter and scuba gear. If that's not active procrastinating, then I don't know what is.

- Mozart wrote the overture for *Don Giovanni* the night before the premiere. There were tickets sold and he didn't have a thing to play. I cannot tell you how good that fact makes me feel.

- Frank Lloyd Wright drafted the plans for Falling Water the morning it was to be presented. THAT MORNING. Certainly, you have time to make cookies.

Procrastibaking Has Made Me a Better Person

While writing a book about baking to avoid doing other things it was impossible for me to bake to avoid writing a book about baking to avoid doing other things. It would've been totally meta to do so; I just ran out of things to make. However, I couldn't just get to work. My slow-windup brain needed to do other things to avoid the task at hand.

In the event that you need multiple sources of distraction, here are some of the pastimes I took up while avoiding writing this book:

- Storm watching
- Smoothie making
- Becoming a *Real Housewives* expert (Oh, who am I kidding—an expert on all things Bravo.)
- Watching makeup and nail art tutorials on YouTube
- Exploring K-Pop
- Listening to too many podcasts to mention
- Soaking my own beans at home to make them from scratch
- Documenting strangers' conversations in coffee shops
  (PS, The most interesting things are said between 7 and 9 p.m.)

If I hadn't procrastibaked in the first place, I wouldn't be writing this book. If I hadn't written this book, I likely wouldn't have explored these new avenues, broadening my knowledge base, expanding my horizons, and improving my eye-shadow blending abilities. Ergo, procrastibaking has made me a better person. I'm confident it can do the same for you. At the very least, you'll have cookies.

After all I've said about the joys of procrastibaking, please keep in mind that this is all in good fun. If at any point you find yourself in real trouble—having a search party sent out to locate you because you haven't left the kitchen in days, your laundry starts moving through the house independently, or a not-so-nice man from the IRS starts sending you daily love letters—maybe throw on the brakes and reenter the realm of productive society. Procrastibaking should offer you a delicious distraction from the daily grind, not get your electricity shut off.

INTERNET FOOD CALENDAR

THE INTERNET CREATED THESE HOLIDAYS AS A GIFT TO OUR KIND. They must be celebrated! All. Of. Them. I've included the most important ones here, the ones that relate to this book! Of course, there are more. Hop down that internet rabbit hole to find out just how many there are.

   Add the hashtag #procrastibakingbook or #procrastibaking when posting your creations so we can hang out. No, not IRL. Online, like normal people.

   Oh, and you can bake for all the regular, nationally and internationally recognized holidays too. You know, like they did in the before time, pre-Instagram.

GLAZED DOUGHNUTS DAY

CHOCOLATE MINT DAY

NUT DAY

CEREAL DAY

WORLD NUTELLA DAY

JANUARY

NATIONAL BAKING MONTH

Um, yeah. The whole thing.

Daily:

2: NATIONAL CREAM PUFF DAY

Show the world just what an over-achiever you really are and make the Classic Croquembouche (page 189).

12: GLAZED DOUGHNUTS DAY

So good you'll have random strangers showing up at your door looking for their morning coffee. Glazed Doughnuts (page 36).

21: GRANOLA BAR DAY

This day will be more fun than it sounds when you make the Granola Bars (page 26).

22: BLOND BROWNIE DAY

Brownies get all the shine, but Salty Sailor Blondies (page 65) and Kitchen Sink Bars (page 57) deserve love too.

24: PEANUT BUTTER DAY

Chewy Peanut Bites (page 42), Peanut Butter Crunch Bars (page 48), Peanut Butter S'mores Bars (page 66)—we got ya holiday right here.

27: CHOCOLATE CAKE DAY

So much chocolate cake to choose from! Chocolate Stout Cupcakes (page 124), Chocolate-Cherry Hi-Hat Cupcakes (page 128), and the Turtle Layer Cake (page 186).

FEBRUARY

CHOCOLATE LOVER'S MONTH

Dark Chocolate Cookie Thins (page 73) will hit the spot.

Daily:

1: BAKED ALASKA DAY

The Baked Alaska Ice Cream Cones (page 173) would be an adorbs way to celebrate.

3: CARROT CAKE DAY

After you make the Tropical Carrot Cake (page 126) they'll be changing the name of this holiday.

5: WORLD NUTELLA DAY

I thought this was every day? Celebrate with Cheesecake-Stuffed Nutella Coffee Cake (page 130).

10: HAVE A BROWNIE DAY

Have all the brownies! Sticky Brownies (page 58), Coconut Brownies (page 59), or Mocha Brownie Cheesecake (page 167).

11: PEPPERMINT PATTY DAY

Feel the sensation with the Peppermint Bites (page 44).

12: BISCOTTI DAY

Almond Biscotti (page 84) feels right.

16: ALMOND DAY

See above. Plus Chocolate-Almond Crunch Bars (page 56).

18: DRINK WINE DAY

Pairs well with baking.

19: CHOCOLATE MINT DAY

Andes candy to the rescue. Double-Chocolate Mint Cookies (page 78).

20: MUFFIN DAY

What's your pleasure? Sweet? Blueberry-Lemon Muffins (page 28). Savory? BEC Muffins (page 29). Healthy-ish? Veggie Chickpea Muffins (page 30).

22: MARGARITA DAY

Pay homage to the frozen variety with Frozen Strawberry Margarita Bars (page 60).

23: BANANA BREAD DAY

Here to serve no matter how many rotten bananas you have, One Banana, Two Banana, Three Banana Bread (page 97).

27: KAHLÚA DAY

Put it in a pie and call it a day. Literally. Spiked No-Bake Cookies-n-Cream Pie (page 133).

PROCRASTIBAKING   10

MARCH

All Month:
CAFFEINE AWARENESS MONTH

When we take time to honor what gets us through the day.

Daily:

4: POUND CAKE DAY
Put other pound cakes to shame with the Black-and-White Loaf Cake (page 108).

7: CEREAL DAY
Show your respect by binding that cereal together with marshmallows in Cereal Treats (page 55).

14: PIE DAY
Throw down with the Caramel Apple Slab Pie (page 148).

19: OATMEAL COOKIE DAY
Raisins not invited. Chai Oatmeal Cream Pies (page 91).

APRIL

All Month:
SOFT PRETZEL MONTH

Because something this good deserves more than just a day, Mall Pretzels (page 164).

Daily:

5: CARAMEL DAY
I don't mean to alarm you, but caramel appears seven times in this book.

14: PECAN DAY
A tart would be smart. Bourbon Pecan Tart (page 140).

20: PINEAPPLE UPSIDE-DOWN CAKE DAY
Since you like to loaf around, Pineapple Upside-Down Loaf (page 110).

25: ZUCCHINI DAY
Enjoy your veggies for dessert with Zucchini-Lime Bread (page 102).

MAY

3: CHOCOLATE CUSTARD DAY

The obvious way to celebrate is to pour it in a cookie crust, Chocolate Pudding Pie (page 138).

11: EAT WHAT YOU WANT DAY

Well, I guess just do what the day says.

14: BRIOCHE DAY

Slather that brioche with sunflower seed butter and cherries on top, Sunflower-Cherry Brioche Buns (page 38).

Daily:

15: CHOCOLATE CHIP DAY

Two cookies and a cake for your baking pleasure. No-Mixer Brown Butter Chocolate Chip Cookies (page 71), Soft Batch Chocolate Chip Cookies (page 80), and Chocolate Chip Snack Cake (page 116).

29: BISCUIT DAY

Make Everything Sweet Potato Biscuits (page 154) and Biscuit Day won't even know what happened to it.

JUNE

4: CHEESE DAY

It's easy being cheesy with Cheddar-Pepper Corn Bread (page 153).

6: GINGERBREAD DAY

Cookie, cake, or house, I've got you covered. Gingersnaps (page 77), Gingerbread (page 99), Gingerbread House (page 192).

Daily:

13: CUPCAKE LOVER'S DAY

School Party Cupcakes (page 122) love you right back!

JULY

3: CHOCOLATE WAFER DAY
Crush those wafers and turn them into crust. They'd want it that way. Spiked No-Bake Cookies-n-Cream Pie (page 133) and Chocolate Pudding Pie (page 138).

9: SUGAR COOKIE DAY
Put the party hats on and make some Strawberry Birthday Cake Cookies (page 87).

15: GUMMY BEAR DAY
Be the only person to celebrate by making yours from scratch, with Gummy Buddies (page 45).

AUGUST

Daily:

2: ICE CREAM SANDWICH DAY
The best part is that my Buttered Pecan Ice Cream Sandwiches (page 171) don't require you to listen to a godforsaken ice cream machine all day.

25: BANANA SPLIT DAY
There isn't a Banana Split Crepe Cake Day yet, but there will be after you make the towering creation (page 176).

SEPTEMBER

All Month:
HONEY MONTH
Happy little Hummingbird Bites (page 69) save the day.

Daily:
9: I LOVE FOOD DAY
Should be obvious at this point.

OCTOBER

APPLE MONTH

Rise and shine with Breakfast Cookies (page 27) every day this month.

COOKBOOK MONTH

Oh, heyyy!

COOKIE MONTH

Literally 20 percent of the recipes in this book.

DESSERT MONTH

Eight out of nine chapters can't be wrong.

Daily:

1: PUMPKIN SPICE DAY

Hats off to all my basic ladies, Pumpkin Spice Bread (page 100).

22: NUT DAY

Sometimes you feel like a Pignoli Cookie (page 76), I never don't.

23: BOSTON CREAM PIE DAY

Donnie, let's make that Bahston Cream Taht (Boston Cream Tart, page 146) to celebrate. It's wicked pissah.

NOVEMBER

Daily:

3: SANDWICH DAY

Your creativity will be on full display when you cleverly celebrate this day with Whoopie Pies (page 93) and Buttered Pecan Ice Cream Sandwiches (page 171).

4: CANDY DAY

There's a chapter for that (page 40).

18: APPLE CIDER DAY

Is there a better way to honor something than by turning it into a doughnut? I think not. Baked Apple Cider Doughnuts (page 32).

22: CASHEW DAY

My grandmother always said, "Those cashews belong in a sheet cake." Blackberry-Cashew Sheet Cake (page 120). Okay, maybe she didn't say that, but she totally would have if she had tried this cake.

26: CAKE DAY

Every day, all day, in my world. Loaf Cakes (page 96), Snack Cakes (page 112). A selection of epic layer cakes, Procrasti-Masterpieces (page 166).

DECEMBER

Daily:

4: COOKIE DAY

Got ya covered.

5: COMFORT FOOD DAY

MAKE ALL THE THINGS

16: CHOCOLATE-COVERED ANYTHING DAY

How about peanut butter balls? Oatmeal Buckeyes (page 70).

17: MAPLE SYRUP DAY

What could be sweeter? Maple Candy (page 46).

23: BAKE DAY

This must be a typo, because every day is bake day.

30: BAKING SODA DAY

Thanks for the lift.

31: CHAMPAGNE DAY

Cheers to you! For someone who likes to put stuff off, you've sure had a busy year baking.

HOW TO USE THIS BOOK

Do I have to read this part?

My answer may come as a surprise to you, but no. I suppose you don't need to read this part. Procrastibakers aren't known to be rule followers, so I understand how reading this section may be perceived as a burden to you. If you're already an expert procrastibaker, then I'm sure you'll figure things out as you go. (Bonus: that takes longer!) On the off-chance you're reading this, here's how to use this book.

Just read the recipes and then make them. Do we really have to belabor this? There's a table of contents in the front and an index in the back; both are lists of everything that's in the book, but different. There's information about the stuff you'll need to bake the stuff and the ridiculous story of why this book exists. There's a bunch of recipes: 100 to be exact. Most of them are pretty easy to execute and all of them are delicious. In each chapter, no-bake and one-bowl recipes are toward the beginning and more complex or multistep recipes toward the end. The last chapter is filled with recipes that are all completely over-the-top. You'll see a few photos here and there.

Scattered throughout the recipes are little tidbits and musings that should help you in your baking process or provide you with more fodder for procrastinating.

TAKE YOUR SWEET TIME

Sometimes we want to meander through the kitchen, and sometimes we sprint through it stuffing the nearest thing in our mouth. There's a handy little alarm clock illustration at the top of each recipe that will let you know approximately how much active prep time you'll need to whip up something scrumptious. I say *approximately* because, by all means, take as much time as you like measuring, chopping, rolling, and scooping. I've purposely left out baking, chilling, and cooling times, since theoretically you could get something else done while those things are happening. Or you could work on that day-to-night eye look.

ROAD TRiP!

Whether it's a trip to the craft store, big-box store, or a website with free two-day shipping, you've got some shopping to do.

KiLL MORE TiME!

Most baking books provide tips that help streamline the baking process, but not this one! Oh no, we're in it for the long haul. Why take the road most traveled when you can wander through the kitchen?

KiLL MORE TiME: BiZZARO EDiT

Sometimes I just can't help myself and I have to share the quickest, easiest way to do something. Please don't hold it against me.

RABBiT HOLE

We've all been there. You come to at 3 a.m. while watching an instructional candle-making video and wonder to yourself, "What did I go online for in the first place? How did I get here? Where are my pants?!" Buckle up, because I'm sending you down the rabbit hole for more baking-related information.

FEED THE MOTiVATiON

You're going to need to get back to whatever it is you're avoiding eventually. These recipes do more than cure your sweet tooth, they're kind of nutritious too!

GAMES!

Fun little time killers like an ingredient word search, doodles, and baking prompts.

Procrasti-Swaps

Procrastibaking doesn't discriminate. It's for the people! And since all of us know at least one person with a dietary need or two or twenty, here are my favorite swaps for a few commonly used ingredients. Also helpful when you've got the itch to bake, but not the stocked fridge or pantry to do it.

FLOUR: Gluten-free flour blends have made leaps and bounds. I like Cup4Cup or the King Arthur blend.

CAKE FLOUR: To replace 1 cup, add 2 tablespoons cornstarch to your measuring cup, then enough flour or gluten-free flour blend to fill the cup.

BAKING POWDER: Swap ¼ teaspoon baking powder plus ¼ teaspoon cornstarch plus ½ teaspoon cream of tartar for every teaspoon of baking powder needed.

BROWN SUGAR: Combine 1 cup granulated sugar and 2 tablespoons molasses for every cup of brown sugar needed.

DUTCH-PROCESS COCOA POWDER: Replace 1 cup Dutch-process cocoa powder with 1 cup unsweetened or natural cocoa powder plus ¼ teaspoon baking soda.

EGGS: Ener-G Egg Replacer is an easy-to-find swap at most supermarkets and big-box stores. If you can't do starches, combine 1 tablespoon ground flaxseeds with 3 tablespoons water to replace an egg in most baked goods. To replace just the whites, use 2 tablespoons chickpea water or aquafaba for every egg white needed.

MILK: In many baked goods, milk can simply be replaced with water, or use your favorite nondairy milk (almond, oat, etc.).

BUTTERMILK: Combine 1 cup whole milk or any nondairy milk with 1 tablespoon lemon juice or white vinegar for every cup of buttermilk needed.

BUTTER: Replace in baked goods with shortening or vegan nondairy spread. In frostings, opt for shortening to avoid altering the flavor.

Things You're Going to Get Sick of Reading

STOP AND SCRAPE DOWN THE SIDES OF THE BOWL.

Because I mean it! Stop the mixer and scrape down the sides of the bowl. I would venture to guess that at least 50 percent, if not more, of baking mishaps start during the mixing process. Valuable little bits of leavener, flavor, and fat get stuck to the sides of the bowl and need to be shown their way back into the recipe. It's your job to help guide them.

ROTATE THE PAN FRONT TO BACK HALFWAY THROUGH.

Put on that oven mitt and get in there and do it! Every oven is different. Every oven has hot spots. Taking the time to show your baked goods around the oven helps ensure they bake up evenly.

POSITION YOUR OVEN RACK(S) AND PREP YOUR PAN(S).

There's nothing worse than wrestling with a piping-hot oven rack because you forgot that you put it all the way on the top when you were making nachos. I'm just trying to help. Also, some of the recipes gotta get going as soon as the batter is done, so prepping your pans first helps ensure everything goes smoothly.

ADD SMALL INGREDIENTS WITH THE BUTTER IN RECIPES THAT INVOLVE CREAMING.

This is something I started doing a long, long time ago. It's a helpful way to assemble a recipe if, like me, you're easily distracted. Most recipes call for combining the small dry ingredients like baking soda and powder with the flour, but how will I remember if I did that after getting pulled away from the mixer by a push notification? Everything's white and fluffy! They're easier to spot when you add them in with the butter. Also, there's no chance of those superimportant little measurements getting locked up in a flour lump if they're evenly distributed during the creaming process.

KOSHER SALT.

This may seem like I'm being overly specific, but different salts have different levels of saltiness. It's a space issue. The large granules of Morton Kosher Salt, the brand I use, take up more room in the measuring apparatus than their teenier Diamond or iodized cousins. I use Morton because it's the most versatile between cooking and baking (IMHO), but please adjust the salt according to the brand and type that you use.

FREEZE-DRIED FRUIT POWDERS.

If you haven't yet explored the world of freeze-dried fruits, you don't know what you're missing. Baking with fresh fruit can be a tricky experience due to the natural variations in sugar and water content. Freeze-dried fruit solves the problem by removing the water. What you're left with is bright, intense flavors that are way easier to work into a variety of baked goods. If you're already familiar with my work, you know that I don't like to use or recommend ingredients or tools that are impossible to find. If I can find freeze-dried fruits at every big-box store and supermarket within driving distance of my rural New Hampshire home, then I'm confident you can find them too. There's also the internet. If shopping for them IRL, check the bulk food aisle, natural foods aisle, nut and dried fruit section, or over by the granola. To turn freeze-dried fruits into freeze-dried fruit powder, simply add them to a large zip-top bag and whack away with a rolling pin until they're pulverized. You can also use a coffee grinder or small food processor. Store the powder in an airtight container in the pantry until the expiration date on the bag.

MEASURE iN CUPS AND OUNCES.

I know, I know. I'm supposed to be giving you obsessively detailed measurements in grams for you to weigh out in your kitchen lab in the name of "accuracy." I've baked professionally for many years and fully understand the need for consistent, accurate measurements in recipes, especially when you bake commercially. But I'm pretty sure you're at home. And I'm certain that you're looking to do something with your hands to relieve some stress and pass some time. Squinting at a digital scale just doesn't do it for me.

I'm not saying to throw things in willy-nilly. Dry and wet measures have their rules. In the name of all that's accurate-ish, please fluff the flour before you scoop and level, pack that brown sugar, and bring your eyeballs down to the wet measuring cup as you pour in the ingredient instead of wobbling it midair.

What I am saying is that measuring with cups and spoons is totally fine to do. I officially give you permission, for whatever it's worth. I've also given you a conversion chart in the back, if you must weigh. You will find your "accurate" as you get a feel for how the ingredients come together, what doughs and batters look like each time you make them, and how your final product tastes. Enjoy the process, and your inaccurate brownie, with all your senses.

Plus your scale could be off, too, and you'd never know it. And my measuring cups don't need batteries. Just sayin'!

TELLING YOU WHAT DONENESS LOOKS LiKE BEFORE i TELL YOU HOW LONG TO BAKE iT. Baking times, in any recipe, are always *suggested*. Dozens of variables can affect how quickly your cake bakes on any given day. Set your timer for half the suggested time, turn your goodie to give it a tour of the oven, then judge how much more time it needs based on how done it is. You'll start to get a feel for how quickly things bake, and soon you'll catch on to the color changes and shifts in smell that are far more important to pay attention to than the timer.

PROCRASTIBAKER'S TOOLBOX

I use a few standard and widely available, but specific, tools throughout the book that you should know about. I put it in a word search for you, because it's more exciting and takes longer to do than just reading about cake pans!

GAME TIME!

```
B E N C H S C R A P E R P A C A K W Y P
N F C W R Z F M G P I I L Z A W J I H M
S J F E M W L A P M E U O F N K N A P S
J N R I X C B T K P T J A V D P G L Q B
R H A C S G Y A A A P P F L Y W N U J A
K E W P N H A N R P W P K T Z A T J K
X F X I E Z S S L B T V A H R P A X I
S Z P I I K R P A G K P N E E G N P G N
D I V C M E A K A R K T A B R M I S I G
P H Y K B D I C D T L X A N M P F T O S
F T Q B W N N F D D U K T D O W F E X H
H C U N G M G A N N I L O Y M G U S O E
W R A D H S N S T N U L A U E V M F N E
G C I J X L Z Q G S T O G P T O M F Q T
B S R A U M B P H B Q Y R U E A Q O O N
H T U R N T A B L E T B R B R L D G C F
H P Y G W N S P O O C S N O I T R O P F
L A D S P I T G N I P I P S C Y T Y P F
Y O G V O S C X Y W T J G G E R W B A X
J G O C J A L U T A P S E N O C I L I S
```

FISH SPATULA: The long, thin, slotted fish spatula is delicate, but sturdy enough to make light work of moving cookies from a baking sheet.

OFFSET SPATULA: Get a small one and a large one to apply frosting, pull out slices, or loosen cakes from the pan.

SILICONE SPATULA: Use the heatproof variety so it doesn't melt in your food.

BENCH SCRAPER: Pick one up with a handle and long, flat blade. Fat Girl Cakes makes the best ones.

PORTION SCOOPS: Grab a commercial set online (with the different-colored handles) to make portioning dough a breeze.

PIPING BAGS: Newer, reusable ones made of silicone work well and are easy to clean.

PIPING TIPS: Large round and large star tips come in handy most often.

CANDY THERMOMETER: The ones that clip to the side are okay, but not the easiest to read. Invest in a digital candy thermometer for quicker, instantly readable results.

BAKING DISH: I use a 13 x 9-inch rectangular dish or pan when making bars and sheet cakes.

BAKING SHEET: My preference is for light-colored, rimmed baking sheets, because they're sturdier and more versatile.

TART PAN: A fluted 9-inch round is the size I use in this book.

ROUND CAKE PANS: Use pans light in color with tall sides in 6-inch or 8-inch rounds.

PIE PAN: Use 9-inch round, standard depth, in stainless steel. Disposable pie pans are too floppy, and thick glass or ceramic ones take too long to distribute heat, in my opinion.

SQUARE BAKING PAN: My go-to size is 8 x 8 inches, also called a brownie pan.

MUFFIN PAN: Standard and mini, get sturdy ones that are light in color.

LOAF PAN: I like to bake in the standard, 8-inch loaf pans or 3-inch mini loaf pans.

STAND MIXER: KitchenAid is king. I have strayed at times, but I always return.

TURNTABLE: Invest in a heavy-duty one, like Ateco, if you make a lot of cakes, or pick up a cheap lazy Susan in a pinch.

CHAPTER 1:

Case-of-the-Monday-Morning Treats

iF YOU WERE A DOUGHNUT,
WHAT KiND OF DOUGHNUT WOULD YOU BE?

RISE AND SHINE, MY LITTLE CHICKADEES!

It's a brand-new day full of opportunities to put off what needs to be done until tomorrow. Make one of these scrumptious morning treats to avoid today's first order of business and maybe tomorrow's as well . . .

Serves 6 to 8

Let's get super real here. Look me in the eye: I don't always bake from scratch. Sure, I could make a yeast biscuit dough and wait an hour while it proofs, then divide it into a million pieces and shape each ball by hand. OR I could open a few of these little pop cans from the dairy case, kick my feet up—sorry, I forgot we were being real with each other—frantically try to caffeinate myself while bribing my children to stop bickering with the promise of buttery, cinnamony monkey bites, and enjoy a tasty treat in a quarter of the time. They even make organic pop-can biscuits these days. What a time to be alive!

In most recipes, monkey bread is baked in a Bundt pan. This recipe will also work in a 9-inch Bundt pan, if that's how you'd like to bake it, but I prefer to use a sheet pan or baking dish. The difference: more crispy crust, more gooey caramel-topped bites, and no death-defying hot pan flipping before your eyes are fully able to open. It's good sheet.

32 to 36 ounces refrigerated biscuit dough (3 small tubes or 2 large tubes)

1 cup granulated sugar

2 teaspoons ground cinnamon

1 teaspoon ground ginger

½ teaspoon ground allspice

½ teaspoon kosher salt

Pinch of ground cloves

8 tablespoons (4 ounces) unsalted butter

1 cup dark brown sugar

½ cup chopped pecans (optional)

½ cup raisins (optional)

1. Position a rack in the center of the oven and heat the oven to 350°F. Grease a 13 x 9-inch baking dish or pan.

2. Pop the cans and cut each biscuit into 4 equal pieces.

3. In a large zip-top bag, combine the granulated sugar, cinnamon, ginger, allspice, salt, and cloves. Seal the bag and shake to blend. Add the cut biscuits to the bag and shake to coat. (Alternatively, combine the sugar and spices in a large bowl, add the cut biscuits, and toss to coat with a spatula.)

4. In a small saucepan, melt the butter and brown sugar over medium-high heat. Whisk to combine.

5. Add the coated biscuits to the prepared pan, dropping in pecans and/or raisins (if using) between them as you go. Sprinkle the remaining sugar left in the bottom of the bag or bowl over the biscuits, then pour the melted butter mixture over the biscuits.

6. Bake, rotating the pan halfway through, until the biscuit pieces are puffed and the whole thing looks gooey and caramelly, 20 to 25 minutes.

7. Transfer the pan to a rack to cool for 10 minutes before serving.

8. Monkey bread is best enjoyed shortly after it's baked, but leftovers can be stored for up to 2 days in an airtight container at room temperature.

 Why is it called monkey bread?

GRANOLA BARS
Makes 16 bars

People are particular about their granola bars, so let me tell you a little bit about mine. These are chewy with a bit of crispness, not tooth-breakingly hard and crunchy. They're also not soft, mushy bars with little texture. They're like the baby bear of granola bars, juuust right. Dates add a chewy, pleasant sweetness and remain softer than other dried fruits like cranberries or raisins.

6 tablespoons (3 ounces) unsalted butter

¼ cup honey

¼ cup maple syrup

¼ teaspoon kosher salt

2 cups rolled oats

1 cup oat flour

½ cup unsweetened shredded coconut

½ cup chopped dates

½ cup sunflower seeds

½ cup mini chocolate chips

1. Position a rack in the center of the oven and heat the oven to 350°F. Line a 13 x 9-inch baking dish or pan with foil and grease the foil. Use enough foil so that it sticks up over all four sides.

2. In a medium saucepan, combine the butter, honey, maple syrup, and salt. Cook, stirring occasionally, over medium-low heat until the butter is melted.

3. In a large bowl, stir together the rolled oats, oat flour, coconut, dates, and sunflower seeds.

4. Pour the warm butter mixture over the dry ingredients and stir to combine. Fold in the chocolate chips.

5. Pour the granola mixture into the prepared pan and press it down firmly with wet hands or a greased rubber spatula. Use a small knife or pizza cutter to score the mixture into 16 bars. Doing this before baking will help prevent breakage later. Press the granola mixture down again if it has started to crumble.

6. Bake, rotating the pan front to back halfway through, until the granola is golden brown around the edges, 25 to 30 minutes.

7. Transfer the pan to a rack to cool. Run a knife or an offset spatula around the outer edges while the bars are still warm to prevent them from sticking. Let the bars cool in the pan until the pan is cool enough to handle. Cut the bars along the scored lines while they're still a little warm and pliable. Allow them to cool completely before storing.

8. Store layered between parchment paper or individually wrapped in plastic wrap or waxed paper in an airtight container at room temperature for up to 1 week.

Oats and dried fruit are both great sources of soluble fiber, which helps you stay fuller longer. Unrefined sugars like honey and maple syrup are easier for your body to process and convert into steady-burning energy.

If you can't find oat flour, grind rolled oats to a fine powder in a food processor or high-powered blender. You may also swap in whole wheat flour.

BREAKFAST COOKIES
Makes 18 large or 32 small cookies

These tender and delicious breakfast cookies are a nice change of pace if you're in a cereal or yogurt rut. They also make for a great 3 p.m. pick-me-up to power you through the rest of your day.

2 tablespoons ground flaxseeds

½ cup water

1 cup rolled oats

1 cup whole wheat flour

1 teaspoon baking powder

1 teaspoon ground cinnamon

½ teaspoon kosher salt

¼ teaspoon ground ginger

½ cup maple syrup

½ cup coconut oil, melted

1½ cups grated apples (about 2 medium apples, no need to peel)

1 cup chopped walnuts, toasted

¼ cup chopped dried cranberries

Burn through the tasks you've been avoiding with a pop of the plant-based protein and omega-3 fatty acids found in flaxseeds.

1. In a small bowl, whisk together the flaxseeds and water. Set aside to thicken while you assemble the rest of the ingredients.

2. Position a rack in the center of the oven and heat the oven to 350°F. Line a rimmed baking sheet with parchment paper or a silicone baking mat.

3. In a large bowl, whisk together the oats, flour, baking powder, cinnamon, salt, and ginger.

4. In a smaller bowl or large glass measuring cup, whisk together the maple syrup, oil, and flaxseed mixture.

5. Pour the wet ingredients into the dry and stir to combine. Add the apples, walnuts, and cranberries and mix to incorporate.

6. Scoop the dough into 1½-inch balls (0.75-ounce scoop or 1½ tablespoons) for small cookies or 3-inch balls (1.5-ounce scoop or 3 tablespoons) for larger cookies. Arrange on the prepared baking sheet 2 to 3 inches apart. Use wet fingers or the bottom of a glass to press down the tops of the cookies to break up the scooped shape.

7. Bake, rotating the pan front to back halfway through, until the edges are golden brown and firm, 10 to 12 minutes for small cookies and 12 to 15 minutes for large cookies.

8. Allow the cookies to cool on the pan before transferring to a rack to finish cooling.

9. Store in an airtight container at room temperature for up to 2 days, or in the fridge for up to 1 week. Alternatively, freeze for up to 3 months and pull cookies to thaw in the fridge the night before you want to eat them for breakfast.

BLUEBERRY-LEMON MUFFINS
Makes 18 muffins

These muffins are classic breakfast fare at its finest. If you aren't into blueberries, or don't have them on hand, swap in any of your favorite berries or finely chopped fruit in equal parts. Same goes for the lemon; leave it out or use a different citrus zest. If you're planning ahead, you can make the batter without the berries and store it in the fridge overnight. In the morning, let the batter come to room temperature and fold in the berries shortly before baking.

4 cups all-purpose flour

2 tablespoons baking powder

1 teaspoon kosher salt

2 large eggs

1 cup granulated sugar

1½ sticks (6 ounces) unsalted butter, melted

1 cup whole-milk Greek yogurt or sour cream

1½ cups buttermilk

1 teaspoon pure vanilla extract

1 tablespoon grated lemon zest

3 cups blueberries

3 tablespoons turbinado sugar, for sprinkling

1. Position a rack in the center of the oven and heat the oven to 350°F. Line two standard muffin pans each with nine paper liners.

2. In a large bowl, whisk together the flour, baking powder, and salt.

3. In a smaller bowl, whisk together the eggs and granulated sugar until combined and lighter in color, about 2 minutes. Whisk in the melted butter, yogurt, buttermilk, vanilla, and lemon zest until just combined.

4. Pour the wet ingredients into the dry and fold to combine. Mix just until the last streaks of flour disappear. Carefully fold the blueberries into the batter.

5. Fill the lined muffin cups three-quarters full. Sprinkle the top of each muffin with turbinado sugar.

6. Bake, rotating the pan front to back halfway through, until the muffins are puffed up, light golden brown, and a toothpick inserted in the center of one comes out clean or with a few crumbs clinging to it, 18 to 20 minutes.

7. Transfer the pan to a rack to cool. Remove the muffins from the pan once they're cool enough to handle.

8. Muffins are best enjoyed shortly after baking, but can be stored in an airtight container in the fridge for up to 3 days. My preferred method of storage is to wrap each muffin individually with plastic wrap. To re-warm a muffin, pop it into the microwave wrapped in a damp paper towel for 15 to 25 seconds before devouring.

BEC MUFFINS
Makes 18 muffins

If you don't already know, BEC stands for bacon, egg, and cheese. The greatest breakfast foods of all time, IMHO. For this recipe, skip the fancy slab bacon and buy some that'll cook up extra crispy. These muffins deliver on the iconic BEC flavor combination, but are far more portable and perfect to serve with a larger breakfast spread.

- 4 cups all-purpose flour
- 2 tablespoons baking powder
- 1 teaspoon kosher salt
- 1 teaspoon ground black pepper
- 1 teaspoon dried thyme
- ½ teaspoon granulated garlic
- 8 ounces bacon, cooked crispy and crumbled (about ¾ cup bacon crumbles)
- 4 large eggs, scrambled and cooled
- 2 cups shredded cheddar cheese
- 2 large eggs
- ½ cup granulated sugar
- 1½ sticks (6 ounces) unsalted butter, melted
- 2 cups buttermilk
- 1 cup shredded Parmesan cheese

1. Position a rack in the center of the oven and heat the oven to 350°F. Line two standard muffin pans each with nine paper liners.

2. In a large bowl, whisk together the flour, baking powder, salt, pepper, thyme, and granulated garlic. Carefully fold in the bacon, scrambled eggs, and cheddar until evenly dispersed.

3. In a smaller bowl, whisk together the eggs and sugar until lighter in color, about 1 minute. Whisk in the melted butter and buttermilk until just combined.

4. Pour the wet ingredients into the dry and fold to combine. Mix just until the last streaks of flour disappear.

5. Fill the lined muffin cups three-quarters full. Sprinkle with enough Parmesan to cover the top of each filled cup.

6. Bake, rotating the pan front to back halfway through, until the muffins are puffed up, light golden brown, and a toothpick inserted in the center of one comes out clean or with a few crumbs clinging to it, 18 to 20 minutes. Move the pan to the top rack the last few minutes of baking for an extra-crispy topping. Bake the rest of the muffins while the first batch cools.

7. Transfer the pan to a rack to cool. Remove the muffins from the pan once they're cool enough to handle.

8. Muffins are best enjoyed shortly after baking, but can be stored in an airtight container in the fridge for up to 3 days. My preferred method of storage is to wrap each muffin individually with plastic wrap. To rewarm a muffin, pop it into the microwave wrapped in a damp paper towel for 15 to 25 seconds before devouring.

VEGGIE CHICKPEA MUFFINS
Makes 18 muffins

These are the opposite of the BEC Muffins, but in the best way possible. Plot twist: I eat vegetarian 90 percent of the time these days. I'm definitely not opposed to eating meat; I just personally try to eat as plant-based as possible . . . most of the time. I would describe these muffins as nutritious and satisfying, maybe not necessarily healthy. I believe *healthy-ish* is the word I'm looking for. Chickpeas and chickpea flour offer a pop of protein to start your day, while crispy shallots and cheese help put a little extra pep in your step. The roasted veggies and batter can be held in the fridge separately overnight and combined in the morning shortly before baking.

Chickpeas are an excellent source of plant-based protein and soluble fiber, keeping you fueled and full longer.

ROASTED VEGETABLES

1 cup chopped red bell pepper

¼ cup chopped celery

¼ cup chopped carrots

1 can (15 ounces) chickpeas, rinsed and peeled

Olive oil

Salt and ground black pepper

BATTER

3 cups all-purpose flour

1 cup chickpea flour

2 tablespoons baking powder

1 teaspoon kosher salt

1 teaspoon ground black pepper

1 teaspoon dried thyme

1 teaspoon granulated garlic

2 large eggs

½ cup granulated sugar

1½ sticks (6 ounces) unsalted butter, melted

2 cups buttermilk

TOPPINGS

3 large shallots, finely sliced into rings

Olive oil

Salt and ground black pepper

2 tablespoons cornstarch

1 cup shredded Parmesan cheese

1. Position a rack in the center of the oven and heat the oven to 400°F.

2. Make the roasted vegetables: On a baking sheet, toss together the bell pepper, celery, carrots, and chickpeas with a few tablespoons of oil and a sprinkling of salt and pepper. Roast until the small vegetables have softened and just started to brown around the edges, about 10 minutes.

3. Leave the oven on, but reduce the temperature to 350°F. Line two standard muffin pans each with nine paper liners.

4. Make the batter: In a large bowl, whisk together the flour, chickpea flour, baking powder, salt, pepper, thyme, and garlic.

5. In a smaller bowl, whisk together the eggs and sugar until lighter in color, about 1 minute. Whisk in the melted butter and buttermilk until just combined.

6. Pour the wet ingredients into the dry and fold to combine. Mix just until the last streaks of flour disappear. Carefully fold the roasted vegetables into the batter.

7. Fill the lined muffin cups three-quarters full.

8. Prepare the toppings: In a small bowl, toss together the sliced shallots and just enough oil to coat. Sprinkle with salt and pepper to taste. Add the cornstarch and toss to coat the shallot rings. Set the shallots and Parmesan aside but have at the ready. Sprinkle each of the filled muffin cups with a pinch of the coated shallots and a sprinkling of Parmesan.

9. Bake, rotating the pan front to back halfway through, until the muffins are puffed up, light golden brown, and a toothpick inserted in the center of one comes out clean or with a few crumbs clinging to it, 18 to 20 minutes.

10. Transfer the pan to a rack to cool. Remove the muffins from the pan once they're cool enough to handle.

11. Muffins are best enjoyed shortly after baking, but can be stored in an airtight container in the fridge for up to 3 days. My preferred method of storage is to wrap each muffin individually with plastic wrap. To rewarm a muffin, pop it into the microwave wrapped in a damp paper towel for 15 to 25 seconds before devouring.

BAKED APPLE CIDER DOUGHNUTS
Makes 12 mini doughnuts

We have a magical PYO fruit farm that sells delicious apple cider doughnuts and farm-made hard apple cider on tap 10 minutes from our house. Magical . . . and dangerous. If you can't find me during working hours between the months of June and October, I'm probably there. Freshly picked fruit is at its peak nutritional value. Picking it yourself is light, enjoyable exercise, and as an added bonus, you're benefiting from all that vitamin D from the sun. The doughnuts and hard cider provide the perfect counterbalance to negate all of that good work. These doughnuts are inspired by theirs, but made lighter by baking instead of frying. Enjoy with a bowl of freshly picked berries and glass of hard cider for the full experience.

2 cups apple cider

1¾ cups cake flour

1 teaspoon baking powder

½ teaspoon baking soda

1 teaspoon ground cinnamon

¼ teaspoon ground nutmeg

½ teaspoon kosher salt

¼ cup dark brown sugar

1 large egg

4 tablespoons (2 ounces) unsalted butter, melted

½ cup buttermilk

1 teaspoon pure vanilla extract

COATING

1½ cups granulated sugar

1 tablespoon ground cinnamon

8 tablespoons (4 ounces) unsalted butter, melted

So many opportunities to leave the house here! Stop at a farm stand for fresh apple cider. Run to the craft store or big-box store to grab a mini doughnut pan and a large piping bag.

1. In a small saucepan, cook the apple cider over medium heat until the cider has reduced to ½ cup, about 10 minutes. Set the reduced cider aside to cool. If you accidentally over-reduce the cider, just top off the reduction with enough fresh cider to reach ½ cup.

2. Position a rack in the center of the oven and heat the oven to 350°F. Grease the mini doughnut pan.

3. In a large bowl, whisk together the flour, baking powder, baking soda, cinnamon, nutmeg, and salt.

4. In a smaller bowl or large glass measuring cup, whisk together the reduced cider, brown sugar, egg, melted butter, buttermilk, and vanilla.

5. Pour the wet ingredients into the dry and stir to combine.

6. Fill a piping bag (or large zip-top bag) with the batter and snip the tip of the bag to create a nickel-size opening. Pipe the batter into the pan, filling the rings three-quarters full.

7. Bake, rotating the pan front to back halfway through, until the doughnuts are cakey and golden brown, 9 to 12 minutes.

8. Allow the doughnuts to cool in the pan for a few minutes before turning out onto a cooling rack.

9. Make the coating: In a small bowl, combine the granulated sugar and cinnamon. Dunk each doughnut in the melted butter before tossing with the cinnamon-sugar.

10. Doughnuts are best enjoyed shortly after baking. Leftovers can be stored in an airtight container at room temperature overnight.

 What's the difference between doughnut and donut? I do-nut know . . .

Case-of-the-Monday-Morning Treats

GIANT CINNAMON ROLL SCONE
Makes 8 scones

Scones are among my favorite, go-to, time-killing recipes, but this specific recipe came to me late in the game. I got the idea while scrolling through my Instagram stories watching Hummingbird High blogger Michelle Lopez develop individual cinnamon roll scones for her own book. Lightning struck with the idea to make a giant rolled scone and cut it into layered wedges. Hold up! Scrolling through Instagram resulted in *active* procrastination? Yes. Yes, it did. I immediately dropped everything and got to work. Do I even need to mention these are perfect for brunch?

SCONE

2¼ cups all-purpose flour, plus more for dusting

⅓ cup granulated sugar

1 tablespoons baking powder

½ teaspoon kosher salt

1½ sticks (6 ounces) cold unsalted butter, cubed

1 teaspoon pure vanilla extract

½ cup heavy cream

FILLING

3 tablespoons (1½ ounces) unsalted butter, melted

¼ cup dark brown sugar

2 teaspoons ground cinnamon

GLAZE

1 cup powdered sugar

1 teaspoon pure vanilla extract

2 to 3 tablespoons whole milk

1. Line a baking sheet with parchment paper or a silicone baking mat.

2. Make the scone: In a large bowl, whisk together the flour, granulated sugar, baking powder, and salt.

3. Add the cubed butter to the flour mixture. Pinch and press the butter into the flour until the mixture resembles coarse sand.

4. Make a well in the center of the sandy mixture and pour in the vanilla and heavy cream. Toss and fold until it comes together to form a loose dough.

5. Dust your work surface with flour and turn the dough out onto the surface. Gently knead the dough two or three times to bring it together. Use your hands to press the dough into a rectangle about 14 x 5 inches. Set the dough with a long side facing you. Imagine the dough divided vertically into three equal sections. Carefully lift the section on the right and fold it over the center section. Lift the left-hand section and fold it over the other two layers. When you look at your dough from the side, you should see three layers. Turn the little dough package so that one of the folded edges is facing you. (See illustration next page.)

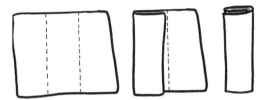

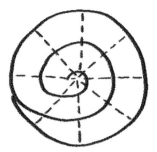

6. Use your hands to press the layered dough back down into a long rectangle similar in size to the first one you made, flouring your work surface and dough as needed.

7. Make the filling: In a small bowl, whisk together the melted butter, brown sugar, and cinnamon. Spread the filling out so that it covers all of the scone dough.

8. Cut the dough lengthwise into four equal strips. Pick up a strip and move it to the prepared baking sheet. Stand the strip on a cut side and roll it up into a coil with the filling side in. Set it in the center of the baking sheet and pick up another strip. Wrap that strip, filling side in, around the coil starting where the first coil left off. Repeat with the next two strips. Gently push the circle of coiled dough down to adhere the strips together and spread the circle out to about 9 inches in diameter. Cover and chill the dough for at least 30 minutes, or up to overnight.

9. Position a rack in the center of the oven and heat the oven to 350°F.

10. Cut the chilled roll into 8 wedges. Imagining the roll is a clock, make cuts from 12 to 6 and 3 to 9, then diagonally between those cuts. Leave the cut pieces together in a circle.

11. Bake, rotating the pan halfway through, until the scones have puffed and browned around the edges, 20 to 24 minutes.

12. Transfer the sheet to a rack to cool for a few minutes before carefully moving the warm scones onto a cutting board or serving platter.

13. Make the glaze: In a small bowl or glass measuring cup, whisk together the powdered sugar, vanilla, and enough of the milk to make the glaze spreadable. If you like your glaze thin, pour it over immediately. If you prefer a thicker glaze, wait at least 20 minutes for the scones to cool.

14. The edges of the scones where you cut them will have baked up together. Tear away individual pieces or slice through the scored lines while the scones are still warm for a more civilized approach. Scones are best enjoyed shortly after baking, but leftovers can be stored in an airtight container at room temperature for up to 2 days. Enjoy at room temperature or reheat the scones in the toaster oven.

Case-of-the-Monday-Morning Treats

GLAZED DOUGHNUTS
Makes about 12 standard doughnuts

The nearest Krispy Kreme to me is fifty-eight miles away, so it was imperative that I learn how to make hot, glazed doughnuts at home. Keep the doughnuts classic, like I have below, or flavor the glaze with melted chocolate, fruit purees, or a splash of liqueur.

DOUGHNUTS

½ cup warm water

¾ cup whole milk

2 teaspoons active dry yeast

3½ cup all-purpose flour, plus more for dusting

¼ cup water

1 teaspoon kosher salt

1 large egg

2 tablespoons (1 ounce) unsalted butter, at room temperature

Oil, for deep-frying (peanut, canola, or shortening)

GLAZE

2 cups powdered sugar

¼ cup water

1 teaspoon pure vanilla extract

1. Make the doughnuts: In a stand mixer fitted with the paddle (or in a large bowl if using an electric hand mixer), mix the warm water, milk, and yeast just until combined. Ideally, the water should be about 110°F, hot to the touch but not scalding. Add the ½ cup flour and mix to combine. Cover the bowl with a towel or plastic wrap and set aside in a warm spot in your kitchen to rest for 30 minutes.

2. Return the bowl to the mixer and add the water, the 3 cups flour, and salt. Mix on low to combine. Add the egg and mix until combined.

3. With the mixer still on low speed, drop the butter into the dough 1 tablespoon at a time. Once incorporated, turn the mixer up to medium and beat for 8 to 10 minutes, until the dough is no longer sticky and slaps the sides of the bowl. The dough will try to ball up around the paddle. Stop and pull it down as needed, so that it doesn't crawl up and around the mixing mechanism.

4. Spray or oil a large bowl. Turn the dough into the oiled bowl and cover. Allow the dough to rest until doubled in size, 2 hours at room temperature or overnight in the fridge.

5. Pour 2 to 3 inches of oil into a deep heavy-bottomed pot or Dutch oven. The oil should not come more than halfway up the sides. It's important to not overfill or underfill the pot. Halfway works great. Turn the heat to medium-high and monitor the oil's temperature with a thermometer. Ideally your oil temperature should be somewhere between 350° and 375°F. The oil temperature will fluctuate as you work, so adjust the burner as necessary. Line a baking sheet with parchment paper or a silicone baking mat and set a cooling rack over paper towels. Have a slotted spoon or strainer/skimmer handy for moving the doughnuts in and out of the oil.

6. Poke down the risen dough and turn it out onto a floured work surface. Roll the dough to about ½ inch thick and cut into 4-inch rings using a biscuit cutter or round cookie cutters. The dough can only be rolled once, so cut the rings close together and save the scraps to fry up as snacks. Move the cut rings and holes to the lined baking sheet. Cover with a clean kitchen towel and let rest for 10 minutes before frying.

7. Place the doughnuts into the hot oil, one at a time, and don't overcrowd the pot. Oil temp drops every time you add something to the pot, so don't fry more than two or three doughnuts at a time. Cook on each side until light golden brown, about 3 minutes per side. Lift one doughnut at a time from the oil, letting excess oil drain back into the pot. Transfer to the rack to cool and set aside to drain while you fry the rest of the doughnuts.

8. Make the glaze: In a small bowl, whisk together the powdered sugar, water, and vanilla.

9. Dip each of the doughnuts in the glaze and return to the rack to allow the glaze to set up. Enjoy the doughnuts immediately. I don't know how to store doughnuts or even what an "extra doughnut" is, so can't help you there.

Love doughnuts, but hate the temperature monitoring and fiddling with hot oil? Run out to the big-box or hardware store and invest $30 to $50 in an electric fryer. It'll monitor the temperature for you.

Case-of-the-Monday-Morning Treats

SUNFLOWER-CHERRY BRIOCHE BUNS
Makes 8 buns

You want a perfect way to start the day? You've got it with these sunflower-cherry buns. Every time I make them I say, "Sun's out, buns out!" I suggest you do as well, because it makes the long process a little more fun. These buns are also the perfect excuse for cutting out a little early Friday afternoon, in order to prep for Saturday morning's breakfast.

Okay, so brioche rolls aren't exactly "health food" by any reasonable standard, but the sunflower seed butter and dried cherries are both good sources of fiber and antioxidants. Or at least more so than butter and sugar alone.

BRIOCHE DOUGH

⅔ cup milk, warmed

1 tablespoon active dry yeast

3½ cups all-purpose flour, plus more for dusting

¼ cup granulated sugar

½ teaspoon kosher salt

4 large eggs

8 tablespoons (4 ounces) unsalted butter, at room temperature

4 ounces sunflower seed butter

FILLING

4 ounces sunflower seed butter

8 tablespoons (4 ounces) unsalted butter, at room temperature

½ cup dark brown sugar

½ cup dried cherries, finely chopped

ICING AND GARNISH

1 cup powdered sugar

2 to 4 tablespoons tart cherry juice

1 teaspoon pure vanilla extract

¼ cup roasted sunflower seeds (or buy raw and toast your own)

1. In a stand mixer fitted with the paddle, combine the warm milk and yeast and mix on low for just a minute to dissolve the yeast. Ideally, the milk should be about 110°F, hot to the touch but not scalding. Add ½ cup of the flour and the granulated sugar and mix to combine. Cover the bowl with a towel or plastic wrap and set aside in a warm place to rest for 30 minutes.

2. Return the bowl to the mixer, add the remaining 3 cups flour and the salt, and mix on low to combine.

3. With the mixer on low, add the eggs one at a time. Turn up to medium speed and mix for 5 minutes more. The dough may want to creep up the paddle. Stop and pull it back down into the bowl as needed.

4. Drop in the butter and sunflower seed butter, 1 tablespoon at a time, and beat on medium for another 5 minutes.

5. Oil or spray a large bowl and transfer the dough to the bowl. Cover and rest in a warm place until the dough has doubled in size, about 2 hours.

6. Make the filling: In a small bowl, combine the sunflower seed butter, butter, brown sugar, and cherries and mash with a fork until combined. Set aside.

7. Coat a 13 x 9-inch baking dish with pan spray.

8. Punch down the dough and turn it out onto a floured work surface. Roll the dough into a rectangle about 18 x 12 inches. Trim any wonky edges straight to maintain a rectangular shape. Brush away any flour that may have accumulated off the top of the dough.

9. Spread three-quarters of the filling over the surface of the dough and the rest in the bottom of the prepared pan.

10. Starting with one of the long sides, roll the dough up into a log. Use a sharp knife to cut the log into 8 equal pieces. Place the pieces evenly spaced into the prepared pan, cut side up.

11. Set the pan aside in a warm place until the buns have risen and started to fill the pan, 30 minutes to 1 hour. At this point you can also wrap the pan and store in the fridge overnight to rise. (If baking from the fridge, pull the pan out when you turn the oven on and let it sit at room temperature while the oven gets to temperature.)

12. Meanwhile, position a rack in the center of the oven and heat the oven to 350°F.

13. Bake, rotating the pan front to back halfway through, until the buns are golden brown and fragrant, 20 to 25 minutes.

14. Transfer the pan to a rack to cool while you make the icing.

15. Make the icing: In a small bowl, whisk together the powdered sugar, cherry juice, and vanilla. Use the smaller amount of cherry juice for a spreadable icing and the larger amount if you want a drizzle.

16. Spread or drizzle the glaze over the warm buns and sprinkle with the sunflower seeds.

17. Store leftover buns in an airtight container at room temperature for up to 2 days. Enjoy at room temperature, or gently rewarm buns in a toaster oven on low.

CHAPTER 2:

Can't-Come-to-the-Phone-Right-Now Confections

iF YOU WERE A PIECE OF CANDY, WHAT KIND OF CANDY WOULD YOU BE?

CANDY-MAKING JUST MIGHT BE A PROCRASTIBAKER'S BEST FRIEND. Caramel doesn't care that the phone needs to be answered, and marshmallow's going to set up whether you blow off that laundry buzzer or not. As a bonus, these recipes yield lots of tiny pieces. Perfect for disguising your work-ditching efforts as sweet treats for friends and family.

CHOCOLATE-CARAMEL MARSHMALLOW POPS
Makes about 12 pops

This is the candy you make when you don't really feel like *making* candy. When using a candy thermometer feels like it would add to the weight of all the things you have to do. It's also a terrific project to do with kids. My inspiration for these pops came from a treat one of our local candy shops makes in at least a dozen different ways. Do like they do and mix up the kind of chocolate you use, and add sprinkles, chopped nuts, or even a little flaky sea salt after dipping the pops in their final coat of chocolate.

1 bag (10 ounces) large marshmallows

1 bag (11 ounces) caramel bits or 40 chewy caramel squares

2 tablespoons (1 ounce) unsalted butter

16 ounces milk chocolate, chips or chopped

1 tablespoon coconut oil or vegetable shortening

ADD-INS

Mini chocolate chips, shredded coconut, toffee bits, flaky sea salt, and/or sprinkles, for garnish

1. Line two rimmed baking sheets with parchment paper or silicone baking mats.

2. Slide two marshmallows onto the end of a lollipop stick.

3. In a small saucepan, combine the caramel and butter and melt over medium-low heat, stirring constantly with a heatproof silicone spatula. Make sure the spatula scrapes the bottom of the pan as you stir to prevent sticking or burning.

4. Dip a marshmallow pop into the caramel and coat on all sides. Tap the stick on the side of the pan to shake off any excess. Set the pop on the lined baking sheet with the stick pointing up and flat end of the marshmallow on the paper. Repeat with half of the pops and place that baking sheet in the fridge to chill while you coat the rest of the pops. Swap the new baking sheet into the fridge and take the first one out after you finish dipping the second batch.

5. Melt the chocolate and oil in a small heatproof bowl set over a pan of simmering water (or in the microwave on high in 25-second intervals, stirring after each, about 1 minute total).

6. Roll one of the chilled pops in the melted chocolate to coat. Tap the stick against the side of the bowl to shake off any excess chocolate. Sprinkle on any add-ins at this point if using. Pick from the ones I've listed above or add your favorite toppings. Set the pop back on the lined baking sheet and repeat with the rest of the pops. Swap the baking sheet with the one in the fridge and finish coating the other pops.

7. Store, layered between parchment paper, in an airtight container at room temperature for up to 2 days or in the fridge for 1 week.

CHEWY PEANUT BITES
Makes 24 "fun size" bars

You might get a familiar feeling when nibbling on these nut bites, because they're a dead ringer for PayDay candy bars. If you've never had a PayDay (seriously, why not?), they're little chewy candy logs encrusted with whole, salted peanuts. They'll be sticky and gooey, but still delicious on the day you make them and much firmer on day two.

4 cups salted peanuts, coarsely chopped

3 tablespoons (1½ ounces) unsalted butter

2 cups peanut butter chips

¼ teaspoon kosher salt

3 cups mini marshmallows

½ can (7 ounces) sweetened condensed milk

½ teaspoon pure vanilla extract

1. Line a 13 x 9-inch baking pan with enough foil to cover the bottom and sides. Coat with pan spray. Spread half of the peanuts out in the bottom of the pan and set aside.

2. In a small saucepan, combine the butter, peanut butter chips, and salt and cook over medium heat while stirring with a heatproof silicone spatula until melted.

3. Add the marshmallows, sweetened condensed milk, and vanilla. Stir until the marshmallows have completely melted.

4. Spread the mixture out in the bottom of the prepared pan. Top with the remaining peanuts.

5. Place a piece of parchment paper on top and press down to flatten slightly and push the peanuts into the candy.

6. Allow the candy to set up completely at room temperature before cutting, 6 hours or up to overnight.

7. Store, layered between parchment paper, in an airtight container at room temperature for up to 3 days or in the fridge for up to 1 week.

These chewy candies have a somewhat redeeming quality thanks to the protein-packed peanuts.

Take these bars OTT with an added drizzle of dark chocolate.

CHOCOLATE-ORANGE CHEWS
Make about 46 pieces

The secret to a chewy, chocolaty candy that tastes similar to the childhood favorite, but better? Orange extract! A little splash into a standard modeling chocolate recipe instantly transforms it into the well-known Tootsie treat. Oh, you don't have a standard modeling chocolate recipe? Sometimes I forget that most of the world doesn't spend their days dreaming up cake designs. In the world of cake decorating, modeling chocolate is a simply made by combining chocolate and corn syrup to form a type of candy clay. The recipe is easy to make, but wrapping the candies individually can be a little time-consuming . . . thankfully.

12 ounces dark chocolate (70% cacao is ideal, but anything over 60% will work), chopped

½ cup light corn syrup

½ teaspoon kosher salt

1 teaspoon natural orange extract

1. Line a rimmed baking sheet with a piece of parchment paper or silicone baking mat.

2. Melt the chocolate in a heatproof bowl set over a pan of simmering water (or in the microwave on high in 25-second increments, stirring after each, about 1 minute total).

3. Remove the chocolate from the heat. Using a rubber spatula, stir in the corn syrup, salt, and orange extract until combined. The chocolate mixture will thicken to a paste consistency.

4. Pour the chocolate mixture onto the prepared pan, cover with plastic wrap, and allow the candy to set up at room temperature for at least 2 hours, or up to overnight.

5. Cut the candy into strips and roll the strips into long logs about a dime's width in diameter. The candy will be very firm as you start to roll it, but will warm and soften under the warmth of your hands. Cut the logs into 1-inch lengths of candy. Wrap the candy in small pieces of foil or waxed paper. Store in an airtight container at room temperature for up to 1 week.

 Who was Tootsie and how exactly did she roll?

 You could pick up precut pieces of foil made especially for candy making at the craft store or in the cake decorating aisle of a big-box store, but cutting your own will take much longer.

PEPPERMINT BITES
Makes about 40 mints

Surprisingly, people have more than a few different ideas on how to make a peppermint patty filling. Unsurprisingly, most taste the same! It is just minty, chocolate-covered sugar, after all. I like this filling version the best, because the evaporated milk adds a bit of creaminess. Try to find food-grade peppermint oil instead of peppermint extract. Extract will do in a pinch, but the oil has a much fresher mint flavor.

1 bag (2 pounds) powdered sugar (7½ cups), plus more for dusting

½ cup evaporated milk

2 tablespoons light corn syrup

1 teaspoon peppermint oil

24 ounces dark chocolate, chopped

1 tablespoon coconut oil

1. In a stand mixer fitted with the paddle (or in a large bowl if using an electric hand mixer), beat the powdered sugar, evaporated milk, corn syrup, and peppermint on low speed until just incorporated. Turn the mixer up to medium-high speed and beat, stopping to scrape down the sides of the bowl, until a smooth paste forms, 3 to 5 minutes. Divide the candy in half and wrap each half with plastic wrap. Place the wrapped candy into a large zip-top bag. (Peppermint oil will scent or flavor anything near it.) Chill for at least 1 hour, or up to overnight.

2. Line a rimmed baking sheet with parchment paper. Dust your work surface with powdered sugar and roll out one of the large candy pieces to ¼ inch thick, dusting the surface with more powdered sugar as needed. Cut the candy into small rounds, 1 to 1½ inches in diameter. Use a small circle cutter, the back end of a large piping tip, or even a plastic bottle cap. Move the cut rounds to the lined baking sheet. Repeat the rolling and cutting process until all of the candy mixture is used up. Freeze the baking sheet until the patties are solid, about 30 minutes (they can remain frozen for up to 3 months).

3. Melt the chocolate and coconut oil in a small heatproof bowl set over a pan of simmering water (or in the microwave on high in 25-second increments, stirring after each, about 1 minute total). Line a rimmed baking sheet with parchment paper or a silicone baking mat.

4. Use a fork to dip a patty in the chocolate. Tap the fork against the side of the bowl to shake off any excess. Slide the coated candy onto the lined baking sheet. Repeat with the rest of the candies, remelting the chocolate as needed.

5. Store, layered between parchment paper, in an airtight container at room temperature for up to 1 week.

GUMMY BUDDIES
Makes about 50 gummy bears

20 MINUTES

There is something very calming and meditative about sitting and filling tiny, individual bear molds with liquid gummy gold. It may seem like it lives on the other side of the tedious, not-worth-it line, but it doesn't, I promise. My kids adore these and I adore the extended alone time it takes to make them.

JUICE VERSION

1 cup fruit juice, chilled

¼ teaspoon citric acid, or 1 tablespoon lemon juice

1 to 2 tablespoons granulated sugar or honey (optional)

3 tablespoons unflavored powdered gelatin

BOXED GELATIN VERSION

1 box (3 ounces) flavored gelatin dessert

1 tablespoon unflavored powdered gelatin

¼ teaspoon citric acid

¼ cup light corn syrup

⅓ cup water

1. Coat silicone gummy bear molds with a thin layer of pan spray and place them on a baking sheet.

2. In a small saucepan or microwave-safe bowl, combine all of the ingredients from whichever version you're making.

3. If using a saucepan, warm the pan over low heat just until the sugar and gelatin have dissolved, 1 to 3 minutes. Stir the mixture frequently with a heatproof silicone spatula to ensure none of the sugar sticks to the bottom of the pan. If using a microwave, cook the mixture for 30 seconds on high, then stir. Cook again for two more 30-second increments, stirring after each one. Remove the pan from the heat or the bowl from the microwave. Skim and discard any foam or bubbles that may have formed while heating.

4. Pour the mixture into a spouted measuring cup or use an eyedropper to fill the wells of your silicone molds. Let the filled molds sit at room temperature for about 10 minutes before moving the baking sheet to the fridge. If you move the baking sheet right after filling, the warm gelatin mixture will slosh out of the wells. Waiting allows the gummies to form a skin along the top, making them easier to move. Let the gummies set up in the fridge for at least 1 hour, or up to overnight.

5. Pop the gummies out of the mold. At this point the gummies are ready to eat, but will have a softer texture than store-bought gummy candy. Store in an airtight container in the fridge for up to 2 weeks.

6. For firmer gummies, scatter the finished gummies on a baking sheet lined with a silicone mat or parchment paper. Leave the gummies out, exposed to the air, for 6 to 8 hours. The citric acid or lemon juice in the gummy mixture acts as a preservative and will keep them safe to eat while you leave them out to toughen up. Gather up the chewier gummies and store in an airtight container in the fridge for up to 2 weeks.

You'll definitely need to hop online and pick up some gummy bear molds . . . and the fruit-shaped ones, and the little robots, oh and . . .

MAPLE CANDY

Makes various amounts (depending on the mold), about 1 cup of candy total

First things first: there's only one ingredient in this recipe. Which means it is of vital importance to use exactly what the recipe calls for: pure, 100 percent real maple syrup. Here in New Hampshire we're fortunate enough to have that available virtually everywhere, even at gas stations. I encourage you to seek it out wherever you can find it near you or pick it up online from a producer who ships. It's more expensive than the maple-flavored-whatever they try to pass off as syrup, but it's worth every cent. The amount of candy this recipe makes will depend on the size of your molds. I like to make tiny candies you can pop in your mouth in a single bite.

2 cups pure maple syrup

1. Set a silicone mold on a baking sheet and coat the mold with a thin layer of pan spray.

2. In a large saucepan, cook the syrup over medium-high heat, stirring occasionally with a heatproof silicone spatula, until the syrup reaches soft-ball stage, 235°F on a candy thermometer. Make sure the spatula scrapes the bottom of the pan as you stir to prevent any of the syrup from sticking.

3. Remove the pan from the heat and without stirring, allow the pan to cool to 175°F.

4. Vigorously stir the cooked syrup until it gets lighter in color and starts to thicken, just a few minutes.

5. Pour the candy into the molds. You may need to press it in with your fingertips as the candy cools. Tap the baking sheet on your work surface to release air bubbles. If you don't have molds, drop the warm candy into dime-size blobs on a lined baking sheet. Allow the candies to cool completely before unmolding.

6. Store in an airtight container at room temperature for up to 2 weeks.

Who got the big idea to boil tree juice and pour it over pancakes?

As candy goes, this is one you can feel good about. Pure maple syrup is your less processed, more nutritious sweet friend that won't leave you feeling like you've got the shakes after nibbling on a few candies.

SUNFLOWER TOFFEE
Makes about 8 ounces toffee

I turn to this recipe more often than I'd like to admit, because it's just so versatile and easy to make. You probably have the ingredients on hand already. Toffee can sometimes be sticky or tough to chew, but this recipe makes a candy that is glossy, crunchy, and smooth. Most classic toffee recipes call for the addition of almonds, but my favorite add-in is sunflower seeds. They add a nutty richness while remaining safe for those with allergies. Julia Moskin liked it so much, she included the toffee (sans sunflower seeds) in the Kitchen Sink Cookies recipe that accompanied the procrastibaking article in the *New York Times*.

8 tablespoons (4 ounces) unsalted butter

1 cup granulated sugar

1 teaspoon kosher salt

1 cup sunflower seeds (or your favorite nut or seed)

1. Line a rimmed baking sheet with parchment paper or a silicone baking mat.

2. In a small saucepan, combine the butter, sugar, and salt. Cook over medium-high heat, whisking occasionally, until golden and bubbling, 5 to 7 minutes. Remove the pan from the heat and stir in the sunflower seeds. Pour onto the prepared baking sheet and spread to about ¼ inch thick.

3. Allow the toffee to cool completely before breaking into chunks or chopping. Store in an airtight container at room temperature for up to 2 weeks.

Dip individual shards of toffee in melted chocolate or coat the whole slab before breaking into pieces.

PEANUT BUTTER CRUNCH BARS
Makes about 18 "fun size" bars

Crispity, crunchity, peanut-buttery, peanut butter crunch candy bars. Yeah, doesn't have the same ring to it as the Butterfinger commercial, but it sure does taste similar. It's long been my favorite candy bar. I spent many hours searching and testing to get to what I feel is as close to the real thing as possible, but homemade.

1 cup granulated sugar

⅓ cup light corn syrup

⅓ cup water

1 teaspoon kosher salt

1 cup creamy peanut butter

4 ounces milk chocolate, melted

1. Line a rimmed baking sheet with foil and coat the foil with pan spray.

2. In a medium saucepan, combine the sugar, corn syrup, water, and salt. Cook over medium-high heat until the mixture reaches hard-crack stage, 300°F on a candy thermometer, about 10 minutes.

3. Remove from the heat and whisk in the creamy peanut butter until smooth. Pour onto the prepared baking sheet and spread the hot candy to about ½ inch thick. It won't fill the pan.

4. Grease the blade of a chef's knife and cut the candy into 1 x 1½-inch bars while it's still warm and pliable. Don't pull the bars apart. Let them cool completely on the baking sheet, about 1 hour. Save all the scraggly end pieces to nibble on or crumble over ice cream.

5. Separate the bars on the lined baking sheet and drizzle with the melted chocolate. Chill in the fridge for a few minutes until the chocolate sets up.

6. Store layered between parchment paper in an airtight container at room temperature for up to 1 week.

NEAPOLITAN MARSHMALLOWS
Makes 36 marshmallows

50 MINUTES

Marshmallows are typically a vehicle for something else: hot chocolate, s'mores, cereal treats, etc. With this recipe, they're the destination. I love the way these layered treats look and taste, but if you only have a little time to kill or just prefer one of the flavors, you can make any of the flavors on their own. If you make just one of the flavors, triple the ingredient amounts so that the solo flavor fills the pan on its own.

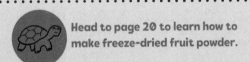

Head to page 20 to learn how to make freeze-dried fruit powder.

Cornstarch, for dusting

VANILLA MARSHMALLOW

¼ cup plus 5 tablespoons water

½ teaspoon pure vanilla extract

1 tablespoon unflavored powdered gelatin

1 teaspoon light corn syrup

1 cup granulated sugar

STRAWBERRY MARSHMALLOW

¼ cup plus 5 tablespoons water

½ teaspoon pure vanilla extract

1 tablespoon unflavored powdered gelatin

2 tablespoons powdered freeze-dried strawberries

1 teaspoon light corn syrup

1 cup granulated sugar

CHOCOLATE MARSHMALLOW

¼ cup plus 5 tablespoons water

½ teaspoon pure vanilla extract

1 tablespoon unflavored powdered gelatin

2 ounces dark chocolate (70% cacao is ideal, anything over 60% will work), finely chopped

1 teaspoon light corn syrup

1 cup granulated sugar

1. Line an 8-inch square pan with parchment paper. Use enough paper so that it sticks up and over all four sides. Coat the paper with pan spray and dust with cornstarch. Tap the excess cornstarch out of the pan.

2. Make the vanilla marshmallow: In a stand mixer fitted with the whisk, combine ¼ cup of the water, the vanilla, and gelatin.

3. In a small saucepan, combine the remaining 5 tablespoons water, the corn syrup, and sugar. Cook over medium-high heat until the mixture reaches soft-ball stage, 240°F on a candy thermometer.

4. Pour the sugar mixture into the bowl of the stand mixer. Turn the mixer on low for just a minute or so to allow the steam to dissipate from the bowl. Turn the mixer up to medium-high speed and whip until light, bright white, and fluffy, about 5 minutes.

5. Pour the warm marshmallow into the prepared pan. Spread the marshmallow out so it fills the pan using a rubber spatula. Grease the spatula with pan spray to prevent the marshmallow from sticking. Set the pan aside while you make the strawberry.

6. Make the strawberry marshmallow: Repeat steps 2 through 4, adding the freeze-dried strawberry powder with the gelatin in step 2. Carefully pour the warm strawberry marshmallow over the vanilla marshmallow. Spread the marshmallow out with a greased spatula. Set the pan aside while you make the chocolate.

7. Make the chocolate marshmallow: Repeat steps 2 through 4, adding the chopped chocolate in with the gelatin in step 2. Carefully pour the warm chocolate marshmallow over the strawberry marshmallow. Spread the marshmallow out with a greased spatula.

8. Dust the top of the finished marshmallow with a light coating of cornstarch. Place a piece of parchment or waxed paper on top of the pan to protect the top of the candy and wrap the pan with plastic wrap. Let the pan sit out at room temperature for at least 1 hour and up to overnight.

9. Dust your work surface with cornstarch or powdered sugar. Carefully lift the layered marshmallow from the pan and place on the dusted surface. Grease a chef's knife with pan spray and cut the marshmallows into 36 squares. Toss the cut marshmallows in more cornstarch to coat the sticky sides.

10. Store in an airtight container, layered between pieces of parchment paper, at room temperature for up to 2 weeks.

SALTED CARAMEL FUDGE
Makes an 8-inch square pan

Making candy is a wonderful way to stay firmly planted in the kitchen, far away from whatever it is you are avoiding doing. You've got to stay close to that thermometer, otherwise all could be lost! In the end, you'll be rewarded with a sweet, decadent confection that's perfect for gifting around the holidays or treating yourself.

CARAMEL

¾ cup granulated sugar

¼ cup water

Pinch of cream of tartar

½ teaspoon kosher salt

¼ cup heavy cream

3 tablespoons (1½ ounces) unsalted butter

½ teaspoon pure vanilla extract

FUDGE

4 cups granulated sugar

1½ cups heavy cream

4 ounces dark chocolate, chopped

2 teaspoons light corn syrup

1 teaspoon kosher salt

4 tablespoons (2 ounces) unsalted butter

2 teaspoons pure vanilla extract

1 to 2 tablespoons flaky sea salt, for sprinkling

1. Make the caramel: In a small saucepan, combine the sugar, water, cream of tartar, and salt. Cook over medium-high heat without stirring until dark amber in color, about 5 minutes.

2. Remove the pan from the heat and carefully whisk in the heavy cream. The caramel will sputter and release steam as the cream is added.

3. Whisk in the butter and vanilla. Set the caramel aside to cool while you make the fudge.

4. Line an 8-inch square pan with enough foil to cover the bottom and sides. Coat the foil with pan spray.

5. Make the fudge: In a medium saucepan, combine the sugar, heavy cream, chocolate, corn syrup, and salt. Cook over medium-high heat, constantly stirring with a heatproof silicone spatula, until the mixture reaches softball stage, 235°F on a candy thermometer.

6. Remove the pan from the heat and stir in the butter and vanilla. Allow the fudge to cool to 110°F.

7. Using an electric hand mixer (or in a stand mixer with the paddle), beat the fudge until it's thicker and no longer shiny, 3 to 5 minutes.

8. Pour into the prepared pan and drizzle the caramel over the fudge. Swirl with the tip of a knife or a toothpick. Sprinkle with flaky sea salt. Chill until firm before cutting, at least 1 hour.

9. Store, layered between parchment paper, in an airtight container at room temperature for up to 2 weeks.

CABERNET CARAMELS
Makes 64 squares

Something special happens when red wine is reduced and cooked into a creamy, chewy caramel candy. Doing so takes ordinary supermarket box wine to levels of greatness. Everyone who has tried these immediately lowers their voice and asks, "OMG, what kind of wine did you use??" Expecting to hear something high priced and hard to find, their questioning face turns to shock when I reply with, "Uhh, those little black boxes." Use whatever wine you like to drink, but rest assured it doesn't need to be expensive or fancy.

2 cups cabernet sauvignon or your favorite red wine

1 cup heavy cream

¼ cup sweetened condensed milk

2 cups granulated sugar

⅓ cup light corn syrup

2 tablespoons water

¾ teaspoon kosher salt

4 tablespoons (2 ounces) unsalted butter

2 tablespoons chopped cacao nibs, for garnish (optional)

1. In a small saucepan, cook the wine over medium heat until reduced to ½ cup, about 10 minutes. Remove the pan from the heat and whisk in the heavy cream and condensed milk.

2. Line an 8-inch square baking dish with enough parchment paper so that it sticks up over all four sides. Coat the pan with pan spray before adding the paper to help it stay put. Grease the paper too.

3. In a large saucepan, combine the sugar, corn syrup, water, and salt and bring to a boil over medium-high heat. Reduce the heat and simmer until the sugar dissolves, about 5 minutes.

4. Whisk in the butter until melted. Whisk in the wine-cream mixture until combined. Cook over medium-low heat. Stir frequently with a heat-proof silicone spatula, making sure to scrape the bottom of the pan as you stir, until the mixture reaches 245°F on a candy thermometer, 25 to 30 minutes.

5. Pour the caramel into the prepared pan and cool completely before covering. Wrap the pan in plastic wrap and chill the caramel for at least 4 hours, or up to overnight.

6. Cut the caramel into 1-inch squares and sprinkle with chopped cacao nibs, if desired. Wrap caramels individually with candy wrappers or waxed paper, or set into candy cups and store in an airtight container at room temperature for up to 3 days, or up to 2 weeks in the fridge.

Dip caramels, one at a time, in melted dark chocolate before sprinkling with the cacao nibs.

Remember the joy you felt as a child upon arriving to school and learning there was a substitute teacher? Knowing that the day ahead would be filled with busy sheets and marginally informational videos. Ah, good times. Recapture those moments and take a stroll through this sweet maze while your treats bake and work waits.

ENTER

DiG iN!

CHAPTER 3:

Better-Late-than-Never Brownies and Bars

IF YOU WERE A LAYERED BAR, WHAT KIND OF BAR WOULD YOU BE?

BROWNIES AND BARS ARE THE PERFECT RECIPES TO TRY IF YOU'RE JUST GETTING INTO THIS PROCRASTIBAKING THING. Fancy layer cakes and pastries attract attention, inquisitive looks from those who might be expecting you to be doing something else. But brownies? No one's going to question brownies. They're just going to say thank you with one hanging halfway out of their mouth.

Sometimes, when I'm on a deadline, I like to play a little game called (say this to yourself the same way the audience says *Wheel of Fortune* at the beginning of the show), "Can You Bind It Together with Marshmallows?" Turn that last letter, Vanna. The answer is yes. Yes, you can! (The crowd goes wild!) Cereal treats aren't just for Krispies anymore. Bind together any of your favorite breakfast cereals with marshmallow for a quick and easy treat that requires no trip to the store. I've made a few tweaks to the original recipe on the back of the cereal box to maximize the crunch and goo factor.

8 tablespoons (4 ounces) unsalted butter

½ teaspoon kosher salt

20 ounces (2 bags) mini marshmallows

10 cups cereal (see suggestions below or choose your own)

1 cup add-ins (optional; see suggestions below or choose your own)

Cereals to Try: Rice Krispies, Cocoa Puffs, Corn Flakes, Cap'n Crunch, Crunch Berries, Corn Pops, Cheerios, Trix

ADD-INS

Chocolaty: Chocolate chips, white chocolate chips, milk chocolate chips, chocolate-covered nuts, chopped candy bars

Sugary: Sprinkles, toffee bits, crushed cookies (Oreos, graham crackers, shortbread), chocolate-covered pretzels, peanut butter chips, butterscotch chips

Healthy-ish: Chopped nuts (pecans, almonds, walnuts, cashews, etc.), freeze-dried fruit, dried fruit

1. Coat a 13 x 9-inch baking dish with pan spray.

2. In a large saucepan or Dutch oven, combine the butter and salt and cook over medium-high heat, occasionally stirring, until the butter has melted and browned bits have formed along the edges and bottom of the pan. Letting the butter brown a little gives the treats an irresistible nutty, caramelly undertone.

3. Add the marshmallows and stir until completely melted.

4. Remove from the heat. Pour in the cereal. Stir until everything is coated with the marshmallow.

5. Pour the mixture into the prepared baking dish and press down with a rubber spatula. Place a piece of parchment paper on top and press down firmly to flatten.

6. Allow the cereal treats to cool before cutting.

7. Wrap individually or store in an airtight container at room temperature for up to 2 days.

Make one of the flavored marshmallow recipes in the Neapolitan Marshmallows (page 49) instead of using store-bought.

NOT SWEET ENOUGH FOR YOU?

For a fruitier flavor, add one 4-ounce box of flavored gelatin or ¼ cup powdered freeze-dried fruit (see page 20) to the melting marshmallow in step 3.

CHOCOLATE-ALMOND CRUNCH BARS
Makes 32 bars

This is a no-bake pantry recipe that tastes like it was made in a French pastry kitchen. You will look like a total sorceress if you slip away to the kitchen and reappear with these in hand. If you don't have almond butter, sub in whatever nut or seed butter you have on hand. Save any crumbles from cutting the bars to sprinkle over ice cream later.

8 ounces milk chocolate

¼ cup almond butter

½ teaspoon kosher salt

5 cups puffed rice cereal

½ cup almonds, toasted and finely chopped

Enrobe the bars in dark or milk chocolate and sprinkle the tops with the crumbs left over in the pan from cutting.

1. Line an 8-inch square pan with foil and coat the foil with pan spray.

2. Combine the chocolate, almond butter, and salt in a small heatproof bowl and set over a pan of simmering water to melt (or melt in the microwave on high in 25-second increments, stirring after each, about 1 minute total).

3. Add the puffed rice and almonds to a large bowl. Pour the warm chocolate mixture over the dry ingredients and stir to combine. Make sure the chocolate coats all of the nuts and cereal.

4. Pour the mixture into the lined pan. Place a piece of parchment paper on top of the pan and press down hard to smush the mixture firmly flat into the pan. Leaving the paper on top, wrap and chill the pan for at least 1 hour, or up to overnight.

5. Remove from the pan and cut into 2 x 1-inch bars.

6. Store in an airtight container in the fridge for up to 3 days.

KITCHEN SINK BARS
Makes 24 bars

There's no excuse for not baking *something*. Scour the cupboards, clear the drawers, and dig up anything that might reasonably belong in a baked treat. I've divided the add-ins into three distinct groups: chocolaty, salty, and found in nature; but don't feel tied to my suggestions. Free-style with whatever you have on hand for a truly unique experience every time you make these bars.

1½ sticks (6 ounces) unsalted butter, melted

1½ cups dark brown sugar

1 teaspoon baking powder

½ teaspoon kosher salt

1½ teaspoons pure vanilla extract

2 large eggs

1½ cups all-purpose flour

ADD-INS

1 cup something chocolaty: chips, chunks, chopped candy bar, crushed cookies, etc.

1 cup something salty: crushed potato chips, crushed pretzels, etc.

1 cup something found in nature: unsweetened flake coconut, chopped nuts, sunflower seeds, etc.

1. Position a rack in the center of the oven and heat the oven to 350°F. Line a 13 x 9-inch baking dish or quarter sheet pan with parchment paper. Grease the paper and sides of the pan.

2. In a large bowl, whisk together the melted butter, brown sugar, baking powder, salt, and vanilla.

3. Add the eggs and whisk until combined.

4. Fold in the flour and 3 cups of chosen add-ins until no flour streaks remain.

5. Pour the batter into the prepared pan and spread to the edges.

6. Bake, rotating the pan front to back halfway through, until the top has lost its glossy sheen and the edges begin to brown, 15 to 20 minutes. Err on the side of underbaking for a gooier experience.

7. Transfer the pan to a rack to cool before cutting, 20 to 30 minutes. Allow the blondie to cool completely before cutting. Grease your knife before cutting into 24 squares to prevent sticking, and wipe the blade clean after each cut.

8. Store in an airtight container at room temperature for up to 3 days.

STICKY BROWNIES
Makes 24 brownies

If you like your brownies dense, sticky, and satisfyingly rich, then this is the recipe for you. Using two kinds of chocolate adds an interesting depth to the chocolaty flavor of these brownies. I suggest storing them at room temperature, but they also taste wonderful straight from the back of the fridge where you've hidden them in an old take-out container to avoid having to share.

4 ounces dark chocolate (60% cacao or higher)

6 ounces milk chocolate

8 tablespoons (4 ounces) unsalted butter

4 large eggs

2 cups granulated sugar

1 teaspoon kosher salt

1 teaspoon pure vanilla extract

1 cup all-purpose flour

1. Position a rack in the center of the oven and heat the oven to 325°F. Line a 13 x 9-inch baking dish with foil, letting the foil hang over all four sides to make it easier to remove the brownies later, and grease the foil.

2. Melt the dark chocolate, milk chocolate, and butter in a heatproof bowl set over a pan of simmering water (or in the microwave on high in 25-second increments, stirring after each, about 1½ minutes total).

3. In a large bowl, whisk together the eggs, sugar, salt, and vanilla. Pour the melted chocolate into the mixture and whisk to combine.

4. Switch to a rubber spatula and fold in the flour.

5. Pour the batter into the prepared pan.

6. Bake, rotating the pan front to back halfway through, until the batter has set and the top develops a cracked, matte appearance, 20 to 25 minutes.

7. Transfer the pan to a rack to cool. Allow the brownies to cool completely before cutting, 20 to 30 minutes. Pop them in the fridge once the pan is cool enough to handle, to speed the process up.

8. Grease your knife before cutting the brownies into 24 pieces and wipe down the blade between cuts to prevent sticking. Store layered between parchment paper in an airtight container at room temperature for up to 3 days. For an even denser, chewier experience, store the brownies in the fridge and enjoy them cold.

COCONUT BROWNIES

20 MINUTES

Makes 16 brownies

These brownies are gluten-free, dairy-free, and refined sugar–free, but not at all short on flavor. The recipe evolved from attempting to bake for a friend following a restrictive FODMAP diet. They're rich, fudgy, and deeply satisfying even if you aren't following a special food regimen.

¾ cup coconut oil, plus more for greasing

1 cup Dutch-process cocoa powder

1¼ cups coconut sugar

¼ teaspoon kosher salt

½ teaspoon pure vanilla extract

2 large eggs

¾ cup white rice flour

2 tablespoons coconut flour

1 cup unsweetened shredded coconut

These gluten-free, dairy-free, refined sugar–free brownies are practically medicinal. Pat yourself on the back, health queen.

1. Position a rack in the center of the oven and heat the oven to 350°F. Line an 8-inch square pan with enough foil to hang over all four sides. Grease the foil with a small amount of coconut oil.

2. In a small saucepan (or in a microwave-safe bowl in the microwave), combine the oil and cocoa powder over medium-high heat just until the oil has melted. (Microwave on high for 30 seconds, then whisk to combine. Return to the microwave for another 30 seconds if needed.) Whisk to combine.

3. Add the coconut sugar, salt, and vanilla and whisk to combine.

4. Add the eggs, one at a time, and whisk to combine.

5. Switch to a rubber spatula and add the white rice flour and coconut flour. Fold to combine.

6. Pour the batter into the prepared pan and spread it level. Sprinkle the shredded coconut over the batter.

7. Bake, rotating the pan front to back halfway through, until the edges appear set and the top of the brownie is matte in appearance, 20 to 25 minutes.

8. Transfer the pan to a rack and allow the brownie to cool in the pan. Grease your knife before cutting into 16 squares to prevent sticking and wipe the blade after each cut.

9. Store in an airtight container at room temperature for up to 3 days.

FROZEN STRAWBERRY MARGARITA BARS
Makes 16 bars

Make these bars in the summer as a cool, refreshing treat or in the winter to pretend you're someplace warm. If you're avoiding something that involves driving, signing important documents, or sharing with children, skip the tequila. If you're making these treats as a sweet reward after slogging through a tedious task, then absolutely add it in.

CRUST

2 cups crushed vanilla wafer cookies (about 80 cookies)

½ cup granulated sugar

6 tablespoons (3 ounces) unsalted butter, melted

½ teaspoon kosher salt

TOPPING

1 bag (14-ounces) frozen sliced strawberries, thawed (or 3 cups fresh sliced strawberries)

1 large lime

¾ cup granulated sugar

¼ teaspoon kosher salt

3 tablespoons white tequila (optional)

1 tablespoon unflavored powdered gelatin

¼ cup cold water

½ cup heavy cream

16 ounces cream cheese, at room temperature

1. Position a rack in the center of the oven and heat the oven to 350°F. Line the sides and bottom of an 8-inch square baking dish with foil. Coat the foil with pan spray.

2. Make the crust: In a small bowl, combine the cookie crumbs, sugar, melted butter, and salt and stir to combine.

3. Spread the mixture out evenly in the prepared pan and press down flat.

4. Bake, rotating the pan front to back halfway through, for 10 minutes. Transfer to a rack to cool completely before filling.

5. Make the topping: Use a microplane or rasp grater to zest the lime and set the zest aside. In a small saucepan, combine the strawberries, lime juice, sugar, salt, and tequila (if using) over medium heat. Cook, stirring with a silicone spatula, for 3 to 5 minutes to melt the sugar and soften the strawberries.

6. Transfer the mixture to a blender (or use a stick blender in the pan). Blend on high to puree and return the puree to the warm pan.

7. In a small bowl, sprinkle the gelatin over the cold water. Add to the pan and stir to melt the gelatin. If the strawberry puree isn't still hot enough, turn the heat back on low for just a minute.

8. In a stand mixer fitted with the whisk (or in a large bowl if using an electric hand mixer), whip the cream and lime zest until soft peaks form, 2 to 3 minutes. Transfer the whipped cream to a small bowl and set aside.

9. Switch to the paddle, add the cream cheese to the mixer, and beat on medium-high speed until smooth, stopping to scrape down the sides of the bowl as needed.

10. With the mixer on low, pour the strawberry mixture into the cream cheese and mix until combined. Scrape down the sides of the bowl as needed. Fold in the whipped cream by hand.

11. Spread the mixture over the crust. Cover and freeze for at least 2 hours, or up to overnight, before cutting into 16 bars.

12. Store bars in a container in the fridge for a creamier, mousse-like experience for up to a day. Store in a container in the freezer for up to 3 months. Transfer to the fridge for a few hours or up to overnight to thaw or enjoy them fully frozen.

CHOCOLATE PEANUT BUTTER OAT BARS
Makes 24 bars

You can feel good about the oats and peanut butter in this recipe . . . and even better about the chocolate. The bars are thin, crisp, and super rich, almost like a candy bar. I suggest storing the bars at room temperature, but I also love these cold, straight from the fridge.

CRUST

1 cup dark brown sugar

1½ sticks (6 ounces) unsalted butter

¼ cup light corn syrup

¼ cup creamy peanut butter

1 teaspoon pure vanilla extract

3½ cups rolled oats

TOPPING

1 cup peanuts, toasted and chopped

12 ounces bittersweet chocolate, chopped

¾ cup (6 ounces) creamy peanut butter

4 ounces white chocolate

These aren't the absolute worst things for you, thanks to the antioxidant-rich oats and peanuts.

1. Position a rack in the center of the oven and heat the oven to 350°F. Line a rimmed baking sheet with foil and grease the foil.

2. Make the crust: In a small saucepan, combine the brown sugar, butter, corn syrup, and peanut butter and melt over medium-high heat while stirring with a silicone spatula to prevent the ingredients from sticking to the bottom of the pan. Remove from the heat and stir in the vanilla.

3. Add the oats to a large bowl. Pour the warm peanut butter mixture over the oats and stir to coat.

4. Pour into the prepared baking sheet. Spread the mixture out to fill the pan and press down with the spatula to flatten.

5. Bake, rotating the pan front to back halfway through, until the crust has browned, 10 to 12 minutes. Sprinkle the peanuts evenly over the warm crust. Transfer the pan to a rack to cool while you make the topping.

6. Make the topping: Melt the bittersweet chocolate and peanut butter in a heatproof bowl set over a pan of simmering water (or in the microwave on high in 25-second increments, stirring after each, about 1 ½ minutes total).

7. Spread the topping out evenly over the crust. Melt the white chocolate in a heatproof bowl set over a pan of simmering water (or in the microwave on high in 15-second increments, stirring after each, about 45 seconds total). Pipe or drizzle the white chocolate in lines over the topping while it's still warm and swirl with the tip of a knife or toothpick.

8. Cool completely before cutting into bars or squares. Store in an airtight container at room temperature for up to 3 days or in the fridge for up to 1 week.

MIXED BERRY CRUMBLE BARS

Makes 36 squares

These mixed berry crumble bars are the perfect thing to make with berries that aren't very ripe or are past their prime. The buttery, lemon-infused crust and crisp, crunchy topping will help make up for anything the berries might be lacking. Use one kind solo, if that's what you've got, or any combination of berries available to you.

Fresh-picked berries are at their nutritional peak. Plus, some time under the sun will boost your vitamin D levels and lift your mood.

CRUST

1 cup dark brown sugar

8 tablespoons (4 ounces) unsalted butter, at room temperature

1 tablespoon grated lemon zest

1 teaspoon pure vanilla extract

½ teaspoon kosher salt

2 large eggs

2¼ cups all-purpose flour

FILLING

1½ cups granulated sugar

2 tablespoons cornstarch

1 teaspoon ground cinnamon

½ teaspoon ground ginger

4 cups fresh mixed berries (blackberries, blueberries, chopped strawberries, or raspberries)

TOPPING

2 cups all-purpose flour

1½ sticks (6 ounces) unsalted butter, at room temperature

½ cup dark brown sugar

½ cup granulated sugar

2 teaspoons ground cinnamon

1 teaspoon kosher salt

1 tablespoon pure vanilla extract

1. Position a rack in the center of the oven and heat the oven to 350°F. Line a rimmed baking sheet with parchment paper. Coat the pan with pan spray before putting the paper down to help it stick to the pan. Grease the paper and sides of the pan.

2. Make the crust: In a stand mixer fitted with the paddle (or in a large bowl if using an electric hand mixer), beat the brown sugar, butter, lemon zest, vanilla, and salt on medium-high speed, stopping to scrape down the sides of the bowl with a rubber spatula to make sure there are no butter lumps, until fluffy and lighter in color, 3 to 5 minutes.

3. Add the eggs one at a time and mix to combine. Stop and scrape down the sides of the bowl.

4. With the mixer on low, slowly add the flour and mix until combined. Stop one last time to scrape down the sides of the bowl and fold in any remaining flour streaks by hand.

5. Bake, rotating the pan front to back halfway through, until the crust has lost its raw sheen and started to brown, about 10 minutes.

6. Transfer the pan to a rack to cool.

7. Make the filling: In a large bowl, combine the sugar, cornstarch, cinnamon, ginger, and berries. Toss to combine, crushing some of the berries in the bottom of the bowl to release their juices.

8. Spread the filling evenly over the crust.

9. Make the topping: In a large bowl, combine the flour, butter, brown sugar, granulated sugar, cinnamon, salt, and vanilla. Press and pinch the butter into the rest of the ingredients until the mixture is sandy in texture. Sprinkle the topping evenly over the berry filling.

10. Bake, rotating the pan halfway through, until the topping is crisp and browned and the berries are jammy and bubbling, 15 to 20 minutes.

11. Allow the pan to cool completely before cutting into 36 squares.

12. Store, layered between parchment paper, in an airtight container at room temperature for up to 2 days, or in the fridge for up to 4 days.

SALTY SAILOR BLONDIES
Makes 24 blondies

One of my favorite ways in the world to avoid getting work done is to get ice cream. It's also a sneaky way to involve your friends and family in your work-avoidance scheme. Who doesn't want to get ice cream? My favorite place to do this is Lago's Ice Cream in Rye, New Hampshire. My favorite ice cream to enjoy while blowing off work is their Salty Sailor flavor. It's a salted caramel ice cream with a salted caramel swirl, studded with bits of chocolate-covered pretzels. This blondie is my tribute to that insanely delicious flavor and also a way to enjoy a taste while they're closed through the winter.

1½ sticks (6 ounces) unsalted butter, melted

1½ cups dark brown sugar

1 teaspoon baking powder

½ teaspoon kosher salt

1½ tablespoons pure vanilla extract

2 large eggs

1½ cups all-purpose flour

¼ cup caramel sauce

3 dozen chocolate-covered pretzels

About ½ teaspoon flaky sea salt, such as Maldon (but add to taste)

1. Position a rack in the center of the oven and heat the oven to 350°F. Line a 13 x 9-inch baking dish or quarter sheet pan with parchment paper. Grease the paper and sides of the pan.

2. In a large bowl, whisk together the melted butter, brown sugar, baking powder, salt, and vanilla.

3. Add the eggs and whisk until combined.

4. Fold in the flour just until no streaks remain.

5. Pour the batter into the prepared pan. Drizzle the caramel sauce over the batter and swirl with the tip of a knife. Scatter the chocolate-covered pretzels evenly over the batter. Dust the top with a sprinkling of flaky sea salt.

6. Bake, rotating the pan front to back halfway through, until it's lost its raw sheen and the edges start to brown, 15 to 20 minutes. Err on the side of underbaking for a gooier experience.

7. Transfer the pan to a rack to cool before cutting, 20 to 30 minutes. Allow to cool completely before storing. Cut into 24 blondies, wiping the blade with a damp paper towel between cuts to prevent sticking. Store in an airtight container at room temperature for up to 3 days.

You could use store-bought caramel ice cream topping to swirl through your blondies, but why not make your own? (See the Caramel Sauce recipe in the Turtle Layer Cake on page 186.) And why buy chocolate-covered pretzels when you could dip them by hand, one by one?

PEANUT BUTTER S'MORES BARS
Makes 24 squares

At the end of the summer and into early fall, when the nights begin to cool, my family likes to end the week with a campfire. No fire is complete without s'mores. The ideal s'more, in my humble opinion, involves a peanut butter cup in place of the chocolate bar. This may seem like blasphemy to traditionalists, but give it a try. The sweet-and-salty peanut butter pairs perfectly with the smoky marshmallow, and there's just enough chocolate to stick it all together. These bars, inspired by that perfect bite, can be enjoyed anytime, anywhere, fire optional.

Skip the scratch baking and use a tube of peanut butter cookie dough for the crust and large, store-bought marshmallows for the topping.

PEANUT BUTTER CRUST

8 tablespoons (4 ounces) unsalted butter, at room temperature

½ cup granulated sugar

½ cup dark brown sugar

½ cup (4 ounces) chunky peanut butter (or creamy)

1 teaspoon pure vanilla extract

1 teaspoon kosher salt

½ teaspoon baking soda

1 large egg

3 cups all-purpose flour

GANACHE FILLING

16 ounces semisweet chocolate, chopped

1 tablespoon light corn syrup

¼ teaspoon kosher salt

1 cup heavy cream

MARSHMALLOW TOPPING

½ cup plus ¾ cup water

1 teaspoon pure vanilla extract

2 tablespoons unflavored powdered gelatin

1 teaspoon light corn syrup

2 cups granulated sugar

1. Position a rack in the center of the oven and heat the oven to 350°F. Line the bottom and sides of a 13 x 9-inch baking dish with parchment paper. Coat the pan with pan spray first to help the paper stick, then grease the paper.

2. Make the peanut butter crust: In a stand mixer fitted with the paddle (or in a large bowl if using an electric hand mixer), beat the butter, sugars, peanut butter, vanilla, salt, and baking soda on medium-high speed, stopping to scrape down the sides of the bowl to make sure there are no butter lumps, until smooth, 3 to 5 minutes.

3. Add the egg and mix to combine. Stop and scrape down the sides of the bowl.

4. With the mixer on low, slowly add the flour until just combined. Stop to scrape down the sides of the bowl one last time and fold in any remaining flour streaks by hand.

5. Spread the cookie dough out to fill the prepared pan. Grease the spatula or your hands to make the job easier.

6. Bake, rotating the pan front to back halfway through, until the edges of the crust have just started to brown, 18 to 20 minutes. Transfer to a rack to cool.

7. Make the filling: In a medium heatproof bowl, combine the chocolate, corn syrup, and salt.

8. In a small saucepan, bring the heavy cream to a simmer over medium heat. Pour the hot cream over the chocolate and whisk to combine.

9. Spread the chocolate ganache over the crust. Transfer the pan to the refrigerator to chill while you make the marshmallow.

10. Make the marshmallow topping: In a stand mixer fitted with the whisk, combine the ½ cup water, the vanilla, and gelatin.

11. In a small saucepan, combine the ¾ cup water, the corn syrup, and sugar. Cook over medium-high heat until the mixture reaches soft-ball stage, 240°F on a candy thermometer.

12. Pour the sugar mixture into the bowl of the stand mixer. Turn the mixer on low for just a minute or so to allow the steam to dissipate from the bowl. Turn the mixer up to medium-high speed and whip until light, bright white, and fluffy, about 5 minutes.

13. Pour the warm marshmallow over the ganache. Spread the marshmallow out so it fills the pan using a rubber spatula. Grease the spatula with pan spray to prevent the marshmallow from sticking.

14. Allow the marshmallow to set up before cutting into 24 pieces, at least 1 hour, or up to overnight. Grease a chef's knife and wipe down the blade between each cut. Toast the marshmallow topping with a kitchen torch or place the bars on a lined baking sheet and toast under the broiler for just a minute. Watch the bars like a hawk to avoid burning the marshmallow.

15. Store in a single layer in an airtight container at room temperature for up to 3 days.

CHAPTER 4:

Cookies. Make All the Cookies.

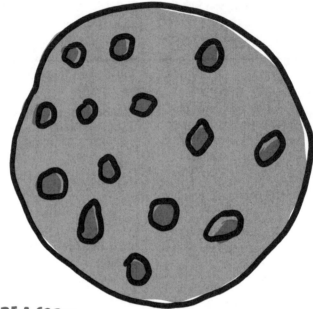

iF YOU WERE A COOKiE, WHAT KiND OF COOKiE WOULD YOU BE?

IF PROCRASTIBAKING WERE A MONARCHY, COOKIES WOULD BE NAMED QUEEN. Holding supreme power over all other baked goods. Time-consuming, check. Fun to make, check. Able to be made with basic pantry staples, check. Share-able, check. Makes the house smell like magic, check plus. All hail the queen!

<... >
</...>
HUMMINGBIRD BITES

Makes 24 bites

20 MINUTES

These chewy, good-enough-for-you bites will leave you buzzing with plenty of energy, just like a hummingbird, to fuel you through even the most arduous tasks. *Hummingbird* also refers to the cake that inspired these flavorful bites.

1 small banana, mashed

1 tablespoon flaxseeds

1 teaspoon ground cinnamon

1 teaspoon pure vanilla extract

¼ teaspoon kosher salt

½ cup (4 ounces) natural peanut butter (or your favorite nut butter)

1 cup rolled oats

⅓ cup unsweetened flake coconut

½ cup finely chopped dried pineapple

¼ cup finely chopped toasted pecans

1. Line a rimmed baking sheet with parchment paper.

2. In a large bowl, whisk together the banana, flaxseeds, cinnamon, vanilla, salt, and peanut butter.

3. Add the oats, coconut, pineapple, and pecans. Fold with a rubber spatula to combine.

4. Scoop 1½-inch balls (0.75-ounce scoop or 1½ tablespoons) onto the lined baking sheet, rolling each ball smooth with your hands.

5. Chill for at least 30 minutes before serving. Store, layered between parchment paper, in an airtight container in the fridge for up to 1 week or in the freezer for up to 3 months.

These bites are loaded with goodness! Protein from the flaxseeds, peanut butter, and nuts. Fiber and antioxidants from pretty much everything in the bowl. You'll be running through walls and blasting through your to-do list in no time, or you'll at least make it off the couch.

Cookies. Make All the Cookies.

OATMEAL BUCKEYES
Makes about 40 buckeyes

Buckeyes are one of my favorite no-bake, pantry-clearing treats, but I always felt they were lacking in a little bit of texture. Enter, oatmeal! Does that mean they're healthy for you? Umm, I wouldn't go that far . . . but you could do worse. The oatmeal adds a nice toothsome chew, but the creamy peanut butter and semisweet chocolate keep these firmly planted in the treat column.

8 tablespoons (4 ounces) unsalted butter, at room temperature

2 cups (16 ounces) creamy peanut butter

1 tablespoon molasses

1 teaspoon pure vanilla extract

1 teaspoon kosher salt

1½ cups rolled oats

3 cups powdered sugar

16 ounces semisweet chocolate, chopped

1 tablespoon coconut oil or shortening

1. In a stand mixer fitted with the paddle (or in a large bowl if using an electric hand mixer), beat the butter, peanut butter, molasses, vanilla, and salt until combined. Scrape down the sides of the bowl.

2. Add the oats and powdered sugar. Mix on low until combined.

3. Line a baking sheet with parchment or waxed paper. Scoop the dough into 1½-inch balls (0.75-ounce scoop or 1½ tablespoons) and place them on the lined baking sheet. Pop the baking sheet in the freezer for at least 30 minutes, or up to overnight, before dipping.

4. Melt the chocolate and oil in a heatproof bowl set over a pan of simmering water (or in the microwave on high in 25-second increments, stirring after each, about 1 minute total). Stir to combine.

5. Insert a toothpick into one of the peanut butter balls and dip into the chocolate three-quarters of the way up. Shake off the excess chocolate and set the dipped ball on the lined baking sheet. Repeat with the rest of the balls. Smooth over the holes left behind by the toothpick with the tip of your finger. Dip your finger in warm water first to prevent it from sticking.

6. Buckeyes can be stored at room temperature or in the fridge in an airtight container for up to 1 week.

NO-MIXER BROWN BUTTER CHOCOLATE CHIP COOKIES

Makes 36 cookies

This recipe started as an experiment to see if I could make chocolate chip cookies with melted butter. Once the butter was in the pan I couldn't help but think that as long as I'm here, this butter would be oh-so-much better browned. And why not add the sugars to the pan to soak up all this brown goodness and melt a little from the warmth of the pan? Every question led to one delicious answer after the next, and eventually to these crisp-on-the-outside, chewy-on-the-inside, thoroughly modern chocolate chip cookies.

2 sticks (8 ounces) unsalted butter, at room temperature

1 cup dark brown sugar

½ cup granulated sugar

1 teaspoon baking soda

½ teaspoon baking powder

1 teaspoon kosher salt

1 teaspoon pure vanilla extract

1 large egg

1½ cups all-purpose flour

½ cup cornstarch

1 bag (11.5 ounces) semisweet chocolate chunks

1. Position two oven racks in the top and bottom thirds of the oven and heat the oven to 350°F. Line two rimmed baking sheets with parchment paper or silicone baking mats.

2. In a medium light-colored saucepan, melt the butter over medium-high heat, stirring occasionally, until it deepens in color from bright yellow to golden tan with little dark brown specks in the bottom of the pan. This should take just a few minutes, so don't walk away. Using a light-colored pan makes this easier to see. Stir the butter or gently swirl the pan until you see the color change. Remove the pan from the heat.

3. Add the brown sugar, granulated sugar, baking soda, baking powder, salt, and vanilla to the pan and whisk to combine. (If you can't use a whisk in your pan—because it's nonstick or it makes you feel like you're hearing nails on a chalkboard—pour the butter into a medium bowl, taking care to scrape out all the browned bits, then add the above ingredients to the bowl.)

4. Transfer the butter mixture to a medium bowl and whisk in the egg. Add the flour and cornstarch to the butter mixture and use a rubber spatula to fold the ingredients together a few times. Add the chocolate chunks and fold until just combined. The chunks will start to melt just a little bit from the warmth of the melted butter. It's perfectly fine, encouraged, and in fact wonderful if this happens. Stop mixing at this point to leave the dough streaked with chocolate.

5. Scoop the dough into 1½-inch balls (0.75-ounce scoop or 1½ tablespoons). Arrange the cookies on the prepared baking sheets 2 to 3 inches apart in five rows, alternating three across and two across—a 3-2-3-2-3 pattern—to ensure they bake evenly.

6. Bake the cookies in batches, rotating the pan front to back halfway through, until the edges have just started to brown, about 9 minutes.

7. Allow the cookies to cool on the pan for a few minutes before moving to a rack to cool completely. Continue baking the remaining dough while the first batch of cookies cools.

8. Store in an airtight container at room temperature for up to 3 days.

Cookies. Make All the Cookies.

COCONUT MACAROONS
Makes 24 macaroons

These macaroons are the little-golden-piles-of-shredded-coconut kind, not the pull-your-hair-out-trying-to-make-meringue-do-things-it-doesn't-want-to-do kind, known as macarons. Troubled coconut macaroons can be dry and flavorless. Happy macaroons, like these, are crispy on the outside and soft and chewy on the inside, with the taste of not-too-sweet, aromatic coconut. Don't skip out on the almond extract. It helps balance and brighten the coconut flavor.

3 cups sweetened shredded coconut

¾ cup egg whites (from 5 to 6 large eggs)

¾ cup granulated sugar

½ teaspoon kosher salt

1 teaspoon pure vanilla extract

¼ teaspoon almond extract

Take the bottoms of cooled macaroons for a little dip in some melted chocolate and drizzle a little more of the chocolate over the tops.

1. In a medium saucepan, combine the coconut, egg whites, sugar, and salt. Cook over medium heat, while constantly stirring with a heatproof silicone spatula, until the mixture turns into a thick paste, about 5 minutes. When ready, it will hold its shape when you press into it with the spatula.

2. Remove from the heat and stir in the vanilla and almond extract. Chill the batter for at least 1 hour, or up to overnight, before baking.

3. Position two oven racks in the top and bottom thirds of the oven and heat the oven to 350°F. Line two rimmed baking sheets with parchment paper or silicone baking mats.

4. Stir the batter before scooping. Scoop the dough into 1½-inch balls (0.75-ounce scoop or 1½ tablespoons). Arrange the cookies on the prepared baking sheets 2 to 3 inches apart. These cookies don't really spread or change shape while baking. Poke them down a little with wet fingers before baking if you prefer a flatter cookie.

5. Bake the cookies in batches, rotating the pan front to back halfway through, until the edges of the coconut start to turn golden brown, 8 to 10 minutes. Flatter cookies will bake faster than rounded ones.

6. Allow the cookies to cool completely on the pan before eating or storing, 10 to 15 minutes. Bake the rest of the batter while the first batch of cookies cools. Store, layered between parchment paper, in an airtight container at room temperature for up to 3 days.

DARK CHOCOLATE COOKIE THINS
Makes about 48 cookies

30 MINUTES

I struggled with what to call these, because they don't quite fit into any existing cookie category. I believe this recipe and my Brown Sugar Crisps (page 75) will join forces to start a new category of cookie called "Butter and Flavor Barely Held Together by Just Enough Flour." Normally, I offer a range of chocolates that will work in a recipe, but this one stands firm at 70% cacao. Any less and they won't hold together well; any more and the bitterness overpowers. Look for bars of chocolate in the candy section of your supermarket rather than the baking aisle.

- 7 ounces 70% cacao dark chocolate
- 1½ sticks (6 ounces) unsalted butter, at room temperature
- ¼ cup granulated sugar
- 1 teaspoon kosher salt
- ½ teaspoon pure vanilla extract
- 1½ cups all-purpose flour

1. Position two oven racks in the top and bottom thirds of the oven and heat the oven to 350°F. Line two rimmed baking sheets with parchment paper or silicone baking mats.

2. Melt the chocolate in a small heatproof bowl set over a pan of simmering water (or in the microwave on high in 25-second increments, stirring after each, about 1 minute total) and set aside.

3. In a stand mixer fitted with the paddle (or in a medium bowl if using an electric hand mixer), beat the butter, sugar, salt, and vanilla until light and fluffy, 3 minutes or so, stopping occasionally to scrape down the sides of the bowl with a rubber spatula.

4. With the mixer on low, pour the melted chocolate into the butter mixture and mix until combined, stopping to scrape down the sides of the bowl.

5. With the mixer still on low, add the flour and mix until just combined.

6. Scoop the dough into 1-inch balls (0.32-ounce scoop or 2 teaspoons). Arrange on the prepared baking sheets 2 to 3 inches apart, because the cookies will spread. I always arrange my cookies in five rows, alternating three across and two across—a 3-2-3-2-3 pattern—to ensure they bake evenly.

7. Bake the cookies in batches, rotating the pans front to back halfway through, until the cookies have spread and lost their raw sheen, 6 to 8 minutes. The smell of warm, buttery chocolate will fill your house.

8. Allow the cookies to cool on the sheet for a few minutes before transferring to a cooling rack. Continue baking the remaining dough while the first batch of cookies cools. Store in an airtight container at room temperature for up to 1 week. My aunt Judy also says that finished cookies taste fantastic straight from the freezer, and I agree.

TURN THE PAGE FOR A DELICIOUS VARIATION ON THESE COOKIES.

Cookies. Make All the Cookies.

DARK CHOCOLATE CUTOUT COOKIES
Makes about 48 cookies

1. Follow steps 2 through 5 in Dark Chocolate Cookies, previous page.

2. Divide the dough in half. Place one portion on a sheet of parchment paper and then another piece of parchment on top. Smush the paper down to spread the dough between the two pieces of paper. Roll your rolling pin over the paper until the dough is a little less than ¼ inch thick. Slide the dough, still sandwiched by the paper, onto a baking sheet. Repeat with the other half of the dough and slide on top of the first batch. Chill for at least 1 hour, or up to overnight.

3. Position two oven racks in the top and bottom thirds of the oven and heat the oven to 350°F. Line two rimmed baking sheets with parchment paper or silicone baking mats.

4. Cut the dough into whatever shape you like. My preference is to cut simple 2 x 1-inch rectangles, but you can do squares, rounds, or any shape that a cutter will cut. Use a small spatula to carefully move the cut shapes onto the prepared baking sheets and arrange them at least 2 inches apart.

5. Bake the cookies in batches, rotating the pans front to back halfway through, until the cookies have spread and lost their raw sheen, 6 to 8 minutes. The cookies will puff and spread a tiny bit, but will maintain their basic shape.

6. Cool and store as for Dark Chocolate Cookies.

 These feel like the perfect excuse to hop in the car and pick up an expensive hunk of chocolate at the gourmet market.

 What exactly do cacao percentages mean? Why are they important?

BROWN SUGAR CRISPS

30 MINUTES

Makes about 30 cookies

You're going to make these cookies and think they're all wrong at many points in the baking process. The dough can't possibly be right—it has way too much butter and sugar. There's no way these cookies are supposed to look like this; they've spread too much and just look all sad and brown. Then, you'll taste one of those wonky, monochromatic, crisp cookies with little bits of buttery lace around the edges and you'll know that everything is just right. If you can't get your hands on muscovado sugar, dark brown sugar will do just fine.

2 sticks (8 ounces) unsalted butter, at room temperature

¾ cup muscovado or dark brown sugar

1 tablespoon pure vanilla extract

1 teaspoon kosher salt

1 large egg yolk

1 cup plus 2 tablespoons all-purpose flour

½ cup granulated sugar, for rolling

What the heck is muscovado sugar and what makes it different from dark brown sugar?

1. In a stand mixer fitted with the paddle (or in a medium bowl if using an electric hand mixer), beat the butter, muscovado sugar, vanilla, and salt until light and fluffy, 3 minutes or so, stopping occasionally to scrape down the sides of the bowl with a rubber spatula.

2. Add the egg yolk and mix until combined, stopping to scrape down the sides of the bowl.

3. With the mixer on low, add the flour to the bowl until just incorporated. Refrigerate the dough at least 1 hour, or up to overnight, before baking.

4. Position a rack in the center of the oven and heat the oven to 350°F. Line two rimmed baking sheets with parchment paper or silicone baking mats.

5. Scoop the dough into 1½-inch balls (0.75-ounce scoop or 1½ tablespoons) and roll the balls in the granulated sugar to coat. Arrange the coated cookies on the prepared baking sheets 2 to 3 inches apart. These cookies will spread as they bake. I arrange my cookies in five rows, alternating three across and two across—a 3-2-3-2-3 pattern—to ensure they bake evenly. Flatten the cookies to about ¼ inch thick using the palm of your hand or the bottom of a drinking glass.

6. Bake, rotating the pans front to back halfway through, until the cookies have spread and are golden brown, 8 to 10 minutes.

7. Allow the cookies to cool on the sheet for a few minutes before transferring them to a cooling rack.

8. Store in an airtight container, layered between parchment paper, for up to 3 days.

Cookies. Make All the Cookies.

PIGNOLI COOKIES
Makes 36 cookies

These were my dad's favorite cookies. I'm so glad I get to put them in a book! He would have really loved that. His literate, food-loving, quick-witted DNA is a big reason I'm able to do this sort of thing. He had celiac disease before #glutenfree was cool and gluten-free flour blends were widely available in supermarkets. These were a sweet treat that I could offer him without having to tweak the recipe one bit.

- 8 ounces almond paste
- 1 cup granulated sugar
- ½ teaspoon kosher salt
- 2 large egg whites
- 8 ounces pine nuts, for rolling

I'm fairly certain you don't have almond paste or pine nuts in the pantry, so it's time for a trip to the store!

1. In a stand mixer fitted with the paddle (or in a large bowl if using an electric hand mixer), beat the almond paste, sugar, and salt at medium-high speed until completely combined and smooth, about 5 minutes. The mixture will appear a little sandy, but no identifiable chunks of almond paste should remain. Stop to scrape down the sides of the bowl with a rubber spatula as needed. Note: Some brands of almond paste can be a little firm. Try kneading the paste on your countertop or warming it in the microwave for 15 seconds to soften it a little before adding to the bowl if needed.

2. Turn the mixer to low speed and slowly add the egg whites until just combined. Scrape down the sides of the bowl one last time and fold in any unincorporated egg white by hand. Chill the dough for at least 1 hour, or up to overnight, before baking.

3. Position two oven racks in the top and bottom thirds of the oven and heat the oven to 350°F. Line two rimmed baking sheets with parchment paper or silicone baking mats.

4. Scoop the dough into 1-inch balls (0.32-ounce scoop or 2 teaspoons). Roll the scoops in pine nuts and arrange on the prepared baking sheets 2 to 3 inches apart. I always arrange my cookies in five rows, alternating three across and two across—a 3-2-3-2-3 pattern—to ensure they bake evenly.

5. Bake the cookies in batches, rotating the pans front to back halfway through, until they start to brown around the edges, 15 to 20 minutes.

6. Allow the cookies to cool on the pan for 5 minutes before transferring to a cooling rack. Continue baking the remaining dough while the first batch of cookies cools.

7. Store in an airtight container at room temperature for up to 3 days.

30 MINUTES

You don't have to wait until the holiday season to enjoy these crisp, chewy, spiced cookies. They're perfect any time of year dunked in a hot cup of coffee or tea or tall glass of cold milk. Swap in honey if you don't have molasses on hand. The cookies will be lighter in color and flavor, but still delicious.

1½ sticks (6 ounces) unsalted butter, at room temperature

1 cup dark brown sugar

¼ cup molasses

2 teaspoons baking soda

¼ teaspoon kosher salt

1 teaspoon ground cinnamon

1 teaspoon ground ginger

½ teaspoon ground cloves

1 large egg

1¼ cups all-purpose flour

1 cup turbinado sugar, for rolling

1. Position two oven racks in the top and bottom thirds of the oven and heat the oven to 350°F. Line two rimmed baking sheets with parchment paper or silicone baking mats.

2. In a stand mixer fitted with the paddle (or in a large bowl if using an electric stand mixer), beat the butter, brown sugar, molasses, baking soda, salt, cinnamon, ginger, and cloves on medium-high speed, stopping to scrape down the sides of the bowl to make sure there are no butter lumps, until fluffy, 3 to 5 minutes.

3. Add the egg and mix until combined, stopping to scrape down the sides of the bowl.

4. With the mixer on low, add the flour until just incorporated. Stop and scrape down the sides of the bowl one last time and fold in any remaining flour streaks by hand.

5. Scoop the dough into 1½-inch balls (0.75-ounce scoop or 1½ tablespoons). Roll each ball in turbinado sugar to coat. Arrange on the prepared baking sheets spaced 2 to 3 inches apart in five rows, alternating three across and two across—a 3-2-3-2-3 pattern—to ensure they bake evenly.

6. Bake the cookies in batches, rotating the pans front to back halfway through, until the edges are set and tops have begun to crack, 10 to 12 minutes.

7. Allow the cookies to cool on the pan for a few minutes before transferring to a rack to finish cooling. Continue baking the remaining dough while the first batch of cookies cools.

8. Store in an airtight container at room temperature for up to 3 days.

DOUBLE-CHOCOLATE MINT COOKIES
Makes 26 cookies

When I was in high school, my friend Gregg came over and ate an entire bag of Andes candies in one sitting. I'm not sure that you really needed to know that odd piece of information, but I think it speaks to the universal appeal of this classic candy. Good peppermint oil can be tough to track down sometimes, but Andes candies are always available at the supermarket or drugstore, making them the perfect go-to ingredient when you need a chocolate-mint fix.

8 tablespoons (4 ounces) unsalted butter, at room temperature

½ cup dark brown sugar

½ cup granulated sugar

1 teaspoon pure vanilla extract

1 teaspoon baking soda

1 teaspoon kosher salt

2 large eggs

1 cup all-purpose flour

½ cup Dutch-process cocoa powder

1 cup finely chopped Andes Crème de Menthe Thins (about 32 mints)

1 cup chocolate chips

What does creamy chocolate mint goodness have to do with the Andes Mountains, anyway?

1. Position two oven racks in the top and bottom thirds of the oven and heat the oven to 350°F. Line two rimmed baking sheets with parchment paper or silicone baking mats.

2. In a stand mixer fitted with the paddle (or a medium bowl if using a hand mixer), combine the butter, brown sugar, granulated sugar, vanilla, baking soda, and salt. Beat the mixture on medium for 3 to 5 minutes until it's completely combined and appears light and fluffy, stopping to scrape down the sides of the bowl with a rubber spatula halfway through.

3. Turn the mixer to low speed and add the eggs. Mix until combined, then scrape down the sides of the bowl once more.

4. Add the flour and cocoa powder. Mix on low until just combined and streaks of flour and cocoa remain. Remove the bowl from the stand mixer and fold in the Andes candies and chocolate chips by hand until incorporated throughout and there are no more streaks of flour or cocoa.

5. Scoop the dough into 1½-inch balls (0.75-ounce scoop or 1½ tablespoons). Arrange on the prepared baking sheets spaced 2 to 3 inches apart, because the cookies will spread. I always arrange my cookies in five rows, alternating three across and two across—a 3-2-3-2-3 pattern—to ensure they bake evenly.

6. Bake the cookies in batches, rotating the pans front to back halfway through, until the cookies have lost their raw sheen, 9 to 11 minutes.

7. Allow the cookies to cool on the pan for about 3 minutes. Transfer the cookies to a cooling rack until completely cool. Continue baking the remaining dough while the first batch of cookies cools.

8. Store in an airtight container at room temperature for up to 3 days.

ROSEMARY-LEMON COOKIES
Makes 34 cookies

One of my all-time favorite excuses for taking a break from work is to run down to my favorite tea shop, White Heron, in Portsmouth, New Hampshire. These cookies are inspired by ones my son and I like to enjoy when stopping in. They're crisp on the outside and chewy on the inside, with a bright, herby floral flavor that pairs perfectly with a cup of tea.

2 tablespoons whole milk

1 tablespoon lemon juice

1 teaspoon pure vanilla extract

8 tablespoons (4 ounces) unsalted butter, at room temperature

1½ cups granulated sugar, plus more for rolling

1 teaspoon baking soda

½ teaspoon baking powder

½ teaspoon kosher salt

Grated zest of 1 lemon

1½ teaspoons finely chopped fresh rosemary

1 large egg

2⅔ cups all-purpose flour

1. Position two oven racks in the top and bottom thirds of the oven and heat the oven to 350°F. Line two rimmed baking sheets with parchment paper or silicone baking mats.

2. In a small bowl or glass measuring cup, whisk together the milk, lemon juice, and vanilla. Set aside to allow the milk to thicken.

3. In a stand mixer fitted with the paddle (or in a large bowl if using an electric hand mixer), beat the butter, sugar, baking soda, baking powder, salt, lemon zest, and rosemary, stopping occasionally to scrape down the sides of the bowl with a rubber spatula to make sure there are no butter lumps, until fluffy and lighter in color, 3 to 5 minutes.

4. Add the egg and mix until combined, stopping to scrape down the sides of the bowl.

5. Beat in the milk mixture, scraping down the bowl as needed.

6. With the mixer on low, add the flour until just combined. Scrape down the sides of the bowl one last time and fold in any remaining flour streaks by hand.

7. Scoop the dough into 1½-inch balls (0.75-ounce scoop or 1½ tablespoons) and roll the balls in sugar to coat. Arrange the coated cookies on the prepared baking sheets 2 to 3 inches apart. I arrange my cookies in five rows, alternating three across and two across—a 3-2-3-2-3 pattern—to ensure they bake evenly. Flatten the cookies to about ¼ inch thick using the palm of your hand or the bottom of a drinking glass.

8. Bake the cookies in batches, rotating the pans front to back halfway through, until the edges have started to brown, 9 to 11 minutes.

9. Allow the cookies to cool on the pan for 5 minutes, then transfer to a rack to finish cooling. Continue baking the remaining dough while the first batch of cookies cools.

10. Store in an airtight container at room temperature for up to 3 days.

Cookies. Make All the Cookies.

SOFT BATCH CHOCOLATE CHIP COOKIES
Makes 36 cookies

This recipe makes a version of chocolate chip cookies that even those little elves would envy. They bake up light in color, with a touch of crispness to the exterior and a soft, buttery, chocolaty middle. This is one of the few times you'll see me use light brown sugar. It keeps the cookie flavor closer to the originals we all know and love.

1½ sticks (6 ounces) unsalted butter, at room temperature

2 ounces cream cheese, at room temperature

1 cup light brown sugar

½ cup granulated sugar

2 tablespoons cornstarch

2 teaspoons pure vanilla extract

1 teaspoon kosher salt

1 teaspoon baking soda

2 large eggs

2¼ cups all-purpose flour

2 cups semisweet chocolate chips

Who are those creepy little elves and why are they baking in a tree?

1. Position two oven racks in the top and bottom thirds of the oven and heat the oven to 350°F. Line two rimmed baking sheets with parchment paper or silicone baking mats.

2. In a stand mixer fitted with the paddle (or a medium bowl if using a hand mixer), beat the butter, cream cheese, brown sugar, granulated sugar, cornstarch, vanilla, salt, and baking soda on medium-high speed, stopping to scrape down the sides of the bowl with a rubber spatula to make sure there are no butter or cream cheese lumps, until fluffy and lighter in color, 3 to 5 minutes.

3. Add the eggs and mix until combined, stopping to scrape down the sides of the bowl.

4. With the mixer on low, add the flour until just combined. Stop and scrape down the sides of the bowl. Fold in the chocolate chips by hand.

5. Scoop the dough into 1½-inch balls (0.75-ounce scoop or 1½ tablespoons). Arrange on the prepared baking sheets spaced 2 to 3 inches apart in five rows, alternating three across and two across—a 3-2-3-2-3 pattern—to ensure they bake evenly. Gently press the cookies down a bit with your fingertips to break the mound shape of the scoop.

6. Bake the cookies in batches, rotating the pan front to back halfway through, until the edges have just barely started to brown, about 8 minutes. Err on the side of underdone. The cookies will continue to set up as they cool.

7. Allow the cookies to cool on the pan for a few minutes before transferring to a rack to cool completely. Continue baking the remaining dough while the first batch of cookies cools.

8. Store in an airtight container at room temperature for up to 3 days.

FLORENTINES
Makes 32 Florentines

These pretty, lacey cookies appear much more complicated to make than they actually are. Flat rounds bake up quickly, but you can kill lots more time by making the rolled or shaped variety. Florentines are elegant and exceptionally delicate. Be prepared for a little breakage along the way. Save all of your broken bits and pieces to sprinkle over ice cream.

1 cup all-purpose flour

2½ cups sliced almonds (optional)

2 sticks (8 ounces) unsalted butter

1 cup dark brown sugar

1 cup light corn syrup

1 teaspoon kosher salt

1. In a small bowl, toss together the flour and almonds (if using).

2. In a medium saucepan, bring the butter, brown sugar, corn syrup, and salt to a boil, occasionally stirring the mixture with a silicone spatula to prevent the ingredients from sticking to the bottom of the pan.

3. Remove the pan from the heat and stir in the flour and almonds (if using). Allow the batter to cool at room temperature for 30 minutes before baking.

4. Meanwhile, position a rack in the center of the oven and heat the oven to 350°F. Line two rimmed baking sheets with parchment paper or silicone baking mats. Set aside a rolling pin and/or wooden spoon for shaping the cookies.

5. Stir the cooled batter with a rubber spatula to make sure the almonds are evenly dispersed. Scoop the dough into 1-inch balls (0.32-ounce scoop or 2 teaspoons). Arrange on a prepared baking sheet at least 3 inches apart. Florentines spread quite a bit.

6. Bake one pan at a time, rotating it front to back halfway through, until the cookies are deep golden brown, about 8 minutes.

7. Meanwhile, set the rolling pin or wooden spoon on a kitchen towel close to your oven so it's all set for shaping the cookies as soon as they are done. The rolling pin is for large shingle-style shapes; the wooden spoon (or a wooden dowel) is for making pirouette or cigar-style cookies.

8. When the cookies are done, carefully lift them one by one from the pan and drape over the rolling pin to cool for shingle-style cookies. For pirouette or cigar-style cookies, carefully lift a cookie from the hot pan and quickly wrap it around the handle of the wooden spoon or dowel. Slide the cookie off the spoon and repeat with the rest of the cookies. Continue baking the remaining dough while the first batch of cookies cools.

9. Cookies can be stored layered, between parchment paper, in an airtight container at room temperature for up to 3 days. Be careful to keep the container away from heat sources or the shaped cookies could flatten back out again.

Melt your favorite chocolate and get to dipping, or drizzle dainty swirls on each individual cookie.

Cookies. Make All the Cookies.

GINGER SANDIES
Makes 32 to 36 cookies

Slice and bake your way to happiness with these subtly spiced ginger sandies. Omit the ginger if you're not a fan and want a simple, but still wonderfully buttery cookie. Or swap in chopped pecans or lemon zest, or even trade maple sugar for the sugar. It's a versatile recipe that can be tweaked to meet your tastes on any given day.

1½ sticks (6 ounces) unsalted butter, at room temperature

¼ cup granulated sugar

1½ teaspoons pure vanilla extract

2 teaspoons ground ginger

2 tablespoons finely chopped crystallized ginger

½ teaspoon kosher salt

1½ cups all-purpose flour

2 cups turbinado sugar, for rolling

1. If making scooped cookies (see step 4), position two oven racks in the top and bottom thirds of the oven and heat the oven to 350°F. Line two rimmed baking sheets with parchment paper or silicone baking mats. (If making sliced cookies, the dough has to chill overnight before baking.)

2. In a stand mixer fitted with the paddle (or in a large bowl if using an electric hand mixer), beat together the butter, sugar, vanilla, ground ginger, crystallized ginger, and salt on medium-high speed, stopping to scrape down the sides of the bowl with a rubber spatula to make sure there are no butter lumps, until fluffy and lighter in color, 3 to 5 minutes.

3. Add the flour and mix on low speed until just incorporated. Stop to scrape down the sides of the bowl one last time. Fold in any remaining flour streaks by hand.

4. For scooped cookies: Scoop the dough into 1½-inch balls (0.75-ounce scoop or 1½ tablespoons). Roll the balls in turbinado sugar to coat. Arrange the coated cookies on the prepared baking sheets 2 to 3 inches apart. I always arrange my cookies in five rows, alternating three across and two across—a 3-2-3-2-3 pattern—to ensure they bake evenly. With the palm of your hand or the bottom of a drinking class, gently flatten the dough balls to ½ inch thick.

FOR SLICED COOKIES: Divide the dough in half and roll each half into a log about 2 inches in diameter. Pour the turbinado sugar out on your work surface and roll each of the logs in the sugar to coat. Wrap each log in plastic wrap and chill for 1 hour, or up to overnight, before baking. Logs can also be frozen at this point for up to 3 months. Allow the log to thaw in the fridge overnight before baking. Preheat the oven and prep the pans as directed in step 1. Slice the logs into ¾-inch-thick cookies and arrange on a baking sheet in the same pattern as the scooped cookies, above.

5. Bake the cookies in batches, rotating the pan front to back halfway through, until they have browned slightly and lost their raw sheen, 8 to 10 minutes.

6. Allow the cookies to cool on the pan for a few minutes before transferring to a rack to cool completely. Continue baking the remaining dough while the first batch of cookies cools.

7. Store in an airtight container at room temperature for up to 3 days.

I know meringues intimidate some, but they really are quite simple once you give them a try. The secret is to make sure your tools are all spotless. Any residual grease will prevent your egg whites from whipping up glossy and firm. Once you get the hang of kisses, go wild and pipe things like hearts, swirls, or even someone's name.

3 large egg whites, at room temperature

¾ cup granulated sugar

Pinch of kosher salt

1 teaspoon pure vanilla extract

1. Position two oven racks in the top and bottom thirds of the oven and heat the oven to 200°F. Line two rimmed baking sheets with parchment paper or silicone baking mats.

2. Pour the egg whites into the clean, dry bowl of a stand mixer fitted with the whisk (or a large metal bowl if using an electric hand mixer). Whip on medium-high speed until frothy. Continue to whip the whites while slowly pouring in the sugar and salt. Add the vanilla and whip until the whites form stiff peaks, 5 to 7 minutes.

3. For piped meringues: Drop a large round piping tip (like an Ateco #807) into a piping bag and snip the tip of the bag just enough to allow the tip to poke through (unless you're using a reusable one). Hold the bag in your nondominant hand or place it in a tall glass and fold open the end of the bag. If you'd like to add some color, paint stripes of gel food coloring inside the piping bag. Carefully add the meringue to the bag. Twist the end of the bag to seal. If you're new to piping, clamp the twisted end of the bag shut with a chip clip. To

pipe kisses, hold the bag straight up and down with the tip just above the surface of the lined baking sheet. Apply pressure to create a blob of meringue about the size of a large grape. Release pressure and pull the bag straight up and away. Repeat with the rest of the meringue, spacing the kisses 1 to 2 inches apart. They need a little space between them, but won't spread while baking.

FOR SPOONED MERINGUES: Add a few drops of gel coloring to the bowl and swirl the color through the meringue. Spoon grape-size dollops onto the prepared baking sheets 2 to 3 inches apart.

4. Bake until the meringues are firm to the touch and no longer tacky, 1 hour to 1 hour 30 minutes, possibly longer if it is humid where you live. You should be able to easily lift them from the parchment paper without sticking.

5. Transfer the pan to a rack to cool. If it's very humid or raining, turn off the oven when the cookies are done and leave them in there, with the door propped open, for another 20 to 30 minutes to continue drying out. There isn't any threat of overbaking meringues at this temperature.

6. Store in an airtight container at room temperature for up to 3 days.

For perfectly pretty meringues, head to the craft store or big-box store and pick up some large piping bags, piping tips, and gel food coloring.

Cookies. Make All the Cookies.

ALMOND BISCOTTI
Makes 24 biscotti

I don't drink coffee, but if I did, I would totally eat these while I drank coffee. I eat them while I drink tea! I think you should, too, no matter what your preferred beverage may be. These classic almond biscotti require a lot of starting and stopping, giving you time to get back in small bursts to whatever it was you were avoiding doing.

10 tablespoons (5 ounces) unsalted butter, at room temperature

1 cup granulated sugar

1 cup dark brown sugar

1 tablespoon grated lemon zest

1 tablespoon grated orange zest

2 teaspoons baking powder

2 teaspoons pure vanilla extract

½ teaspoon almond extract

½ teaspoon kosher salt

2 large eggs

2¼ cups all-purpose flour

2 cups almonds, toasted and coarsely chopped

3 tablespoons turbinado sugar, for sprinkling

1. Position two oven racks in the top and bottom thirds of the oven and heat the oven to 350°F. Line two baking sheets with parchment paper or a silicone baking mat.

2. In a stand mixer fitted with the paddle (or in a large bowl if using an electric hand mixer), beat the butter, granulated sugar, brown sugar, lemon zest, orange zest, baking powder, vanilla, almond extract, and salt at medium-high speed, stopping to scrape the sides of the bowl down with a rubber spatula to make sure there are no butter lumps, until fluffy and lighter in color, 3 to 5 minutes.

3. Add the eggs and mix until combined, stopping to scrape down the sides of the bowl.

4. With the mixer on low, add the flour and chopped almonds until just combined. Stop and scrape down the bowl one last time and fold in any flour streaks by hand.

5. Scrape all of the dough out onto one of the prepared baking sheets and form it into a log about 11 x 3 inches. Brush the top of the log with water and sprinkle with the turbinado sugar.

6. Bake on the lower of the two racks, rotating the pan front to back halfway through, until the dough has spread, cracked along the top, lost its raw sheen, and started to brown, 20 to 25 minutes. Leave the oven on, but reduce the temperature to 300°F.

7. Transfer the pan to a rack and allow the giant cookie to cool until it's able to be handled, 15 to 20 minutes.

8. Move the log to a cutting board and use a serrated knife to cut the rectangle crosswise and on the diagonal into long ½-inch-thick slices. Return the slices to the baking sheets, cut sides up. It's okay if the cookies are very close to each other; they won't spread any more. Use a second lined baking sheet if you need to.

9. Bake, rotating the pan front to back halfway through, until golden brown, 10 minutes more.

10. Allow the cookies to cool on the pan for a few minutes before moving to a rack to finish cooling.

11. Store in an airtight container at room temperature for up to 2 weeks.

BUTTERCRUNCH COOKIES

Makes 32 cookies

40 MINUTES

I was introduced to these cookies shortly after moving to New England and it was love at first bite. My affection for them is so strong that they are my absolute favorite thing to bake when I'm supposed to be doing other baking. I shared that tidbit with Julia Moskin as she wrote the procrastibaking article for the *New York Times* and she included the toffee bits in the cookie recipe she had been developing for the article. They are tiny bits of magic that bake into pools of crisp, buttery goodness.

What is toffee? Is it brickle? What's brickle?

TOFFEE

8 tablespoons (4 ounces) unsalted butter

1 cup granulated sugar

1 teaspoon kosher salt

COOKIES

1½ sticks (6 ounces) unsalted butter, at room temperature

1½ cups dark brown sugar

2 tablespoons cornstarch

¾ teaspoon baking powder

½ teaspoon baking soda

1 teaspoon kosher salt

1 teaspoon pure vanilla extract

1 large egg

2 cups all-purpose flour

Cookies. Make All the Cookies.

1. Line a baking sheet with parchment paper or a silicone baking mat.

2. Make the toffee: In a small saucepan, cook the butter, granulated sugar, and salt over medium-high heat, whisking occasionally, until golden and bubbling, 5 to 7 minutes. Pour onto the prepared baking sheet.

3. Allow the toffee to cool completely. Speed the process up by popping the sheet in the fridge to cool while you work.

4. Position two oven racks in the top and bottom thirds of the oven and heat the oven to 350°F. Line two rimmed baking sheets with parchment paper or silicone baking mats.

5. Make the cookies: In a stand mixer fitted with the paddle (or in a large bowl if using an electric hand mixer), beat the butter, brown sugar, cornstarch, baking powder, baking soda, salt, and vanilla until light and fluffy, 3 to 5 minutes, stopping occasionally to scrape down the sides of the bowl with a rubber spatula.

6. Add the egg and mix until combined, stopping to scrape down the sides of the bowl.

7. With the mixer on low, add the flour and mix until the dough is crumbly and still a little powdery.

8. Chop the toffee into ¼- to ½-inch chunks. Scrape the chopped toffee, tiny shards and all, into the cookie dough. Mix on low for just a few seconds to combine.

9. Scoop the dough into 1½-inch balls (0.75-ounce scoop or 1½ tablespoons). Arrange on the prepared baking sheets spaced 2 to 3 inches apart in five rows, alternating three across and two across—a 3-2-3-2-3 pattern—to ensure they bake evenly.

10. Bake the cookies in batches, rotating the pan front to back halfway through, until the cookies have just started to brown around the edges, about 9 minutes. They will appear puffy and not quite done with random toffee blowouts, but this is perfect. The hot cookies will fall and crackle while the pools of melted toffee solidify. Allow the cookies to cool for at least 10 minutes on the pan before moving them. Transfer the cooled cookies to a plate or storage container. Continue baking the remaining dough while the first batch of cookies cools.

11. Store in an airtight container at room temperature for 3 to 4 days. Layer the cookies with parchment paper if you live in a humid area.

STRAWBERRY BIRTHDAY CAKE COOKIES

Makes 32 cookies

Ooooh, I didn't know it was your birthday! Is it your birthday? Maybe it's your half-birthday? Maybe it's your cat's birthday? (What does she know?) 364 days out of the year it's your unbirthday! There's always a reason to celebrate with birthday cake cookies. Look for freeze-dried strawberries in the granola or dried fruit section of your local supermarket or big-box store.

Head to the craft store or big-box store to grab your freeze-dried strawberries, a large star piping tip, and a large piping bag to make these cookies picture-perfect!

COOKIES

1 bag (1.2 ounces) freeze-dried strawberries (about 1 cup)

2 sticks (8 ounces) unsalted butter, at room temperature

¾ cup granulated sugar

1 tablespoon lemon juice

1 teaspoon pure vanilla extract

1 teaspoon baking soda

½ teaspoon baking powder

½ teaspoon kosher salt

1 large egg

2 cups all-purpose flour

½ cup rainbow sprinkles, plus more for garnishing

FROSTING

8 tablespoons (4 ounces) unsalted butter, at room temperature

8 tablespoons (4 ounces) vegetable shortening

2 teaspoons pure vanilla extract

⅛ teaspoon kosher salt

3½ cups powdered sugar

2 to 4 tablespoons whole milk

1. Position two oven racks in the top and bottom thirds of the oven and heat the oven to 350°F. Line two rimmed baking sheets with parchment paper or silicone baking mats.

2. Make the cookies: In a stand mixer fitted with the paddle (or in a large bowl if using an electric hand mixer), beat the strawberries, butter, granulated sugar, lemon juice, vanilla, baking soda, baking powder, and salt on medium-high speed, stopping occasionally to scrape down the sides of the bowl with a rubber spatula to make sure there are no butter lumps, until the strawberries have been pulverized and the mixture is light and fluffy, 3 to 5 minutes.

3. Add the egg and mix until combined, stopping to scrape down the sides of the bowl.

4. With the mixer on low, add the flour until just incorporated. Stop one last time to scrape down the sides of the bowl. Add the sprinkles and fold them in by hand.

5. Scoop the dough into 1½-inch balls (0.75-ounce scoop or 1½ tablespoons). Arrange on the prepared baking sheets spaced 2 to 3 inches apart in five rows, alternating three across and two across—a 3-2-3-2-3 pattern—to ensure they bake evenly.

6. Bake the cookies in batches, rotating the pan front to back halfway through, until the cookies have spread and puffed up, 8 to 10 minutes.

7. Let the cookies cool on the pan for a minute or two before transferring to a cooling rack. Allow them to cool completely before frosting. Continue baking the remaining dough while the first batch of cookies cools.

8. Make the frosting: In a stand mixer fitted with the paddle (or in a large bowl if using an electric hand mixer), beat the butter on its own until smooth and no small lumps remain, 2 to 3 minutes. Scrape down the sides of the bowl and add the vegetable shortening, vanilla, and salt. Beat until the mixture is fluffy and lighter in color, stopping to scrape down the sides of the bowl, 3 to 5 minutes.

9. Turn the mixer to low speed and slowly add the powdered sugar until just combined. Stop and scrape down the sides of the bowl, then turn the mixer up to medium and beat until the frosting is bright white and fluffy, 3 to 5 minutes.

10. With the mixer on low speed, add the milk 1 tablespoon at a time, until your desired frosting consistency is achieved.

11. Spread the frosting onto the cooled cookies and top with more sprinkles. Or fill a piping bag fitted with a large star tip with the frosting and pipe swirls on each cookie. Position the piping tip so that it's just above the center of a cookie. Apply pressure to the bag and move the tip in a circular motion around the center point. Release pressure as you make it back to where you started, and pull the bag down and away from the cookie.

12. Store, layered between parchment paper, in an airtight container at room temperature for up to 3 days.

SUNFLOWER-CHERRY BRIOCHE BUNS (PAGE 38)

Gummy Buddies
(page 45)

Peanut Butter Crunch
Bars (page 48)

Neapolitan Marshmallows
(page 49)

Sunflower Toffee
(page 47)

Chocolate-Orange
Chews (page 43)

Maple Candy
(page 46)

Cabernet Caramels
(page 52)

Peppermint Bites
(page 44)

CEREAL TREATS (PAGE 55)

No-Mixer Brown Butter Chocolate Chip Cookies (page 71)

Pineapple-Lime
Thumbprints
(page 89)

Salty Sailor Blondies
(page 65)

Rosemary-
Lemon Cookies
(page 79)

Dark Chocolate Cookie Thins
(page 73)

Chai Oatmeal
Cream Pies
(page 91)

Butter Crunch Cookies (page 85)

Double-Chocolate Mint Cookies (page 78)

COOKIES. MAKE ALL THE COOKIES. (PAGE 68)

STRAWBERRY BIRTHDAY CAKE COOKIES (PAGE 87)

Pineapple Upside-Down
Loaf (page 110)

Black-and-White
Loaf Cake (page 108)

Pumpkin Spice Bread
(page 100)

Raspberry-Hibiscus
Loaf Cake (page 106)

LATE-FOR-EVERYTHING LOAF CAKES (PAGE 96)

BLACKBERRY-CASHEW SHEET CAKE (PAGE 120)

CHEESECAKE-STUFFED NUTELLA COFFEE CAKE (PAGE 130)

CARAMEL APPLE SLAB PIE (PAGE 148)

EVERYTHING SWEET POTATO BISCUITS (PAGE 154)

BAKED ALASKA ICE CREAM CONES (PAGE 173)

BANANA SPLIT CREPE CAKE (PAGE 176)

SNOWBALL CAKE (PAGE 181)

LEMON-BERRY LAYER CAKE (PAGE 183)

CLASSIC CROQUEMBOUCHE (PAGE 189)

GINGERBREAD HOUSE (PAGE 192)

PINEAPPLE-LIME THUMBPRINTS
Makes 48 cookies

You don't know it yet, but you love pineapple jam! Its bright, tangy flavor is so unexpected and oddly refreshing. Cooking the pineapple with sugar and lime mellows the acidity without losing that familiar pineapple punch. The sweet-tart pineapple pairs perfectly with the crumbly, nutty brown butter cookie it's perched upon. If you're not into pineapple, make the cookies on their own, sans thumbprint, or fill them with literally anything else. Lemon curd, lime curd, a berry jam, ganache, or caramel would all be delicious substitutes.

JAM

2 cups crushed pineapple (canned or fresh), drained

1 tablespoon lime juice

1 packet (1.75 ounces) powdered pectin

3 to 4 cups granulated sugar

Grated zest of 1 lime

COOKIES

2 sticks (8 ounces) unsalted butter

1½ cups powdered sugar, plus more for coating

½ teaspoon kosher salt

1½ cups all-purpose flour

1. Make the jam: In a medium nonreactive saucepot, combine the pineapple and lime juice and bring to a boil over medium-high heat. Stir occasionally with a heatproof silicone spatula to prevent the pineapple from sticking to the sides or bottom of the pot.

2. Stir in the pectin and return to a boil.

3. Stir in the sugar, 1 cup at a time, and bring the jam back to a boil each time. Pour a spoonful onto a plate and let it cool for a second before tasting it for sweetness. Very ripe pineapples will require less sugar, while an underripe pineapple will require the full amount. Continue to taste between sugar additions. Boil until the jam slides off the spatula in smooth sheets, 1 to 2 minutes. Stir in the lime zest.

4. Pour into a clean heatproof container. Store, covered, in the fridge for up to 1 month. At this point the jam can also be canned for long-term storage by following the canning methods required for the jars you're using.

5. Make the cookies: In a light-colored saucepan, cook the butter over medium-high heat, stirring occasionally, until the butter has deepened to a dark, golden color with little browned bits forming on the bottom of the pan. Remove from the heat and pour the brown butter into a heatproof container, being sure to scrape in all of the little browned bits. Chill until the butter has resolidified, at least 1 hour, or up to overnight.

6. Position a rack in the center of the oven and heat the oven to 350°F. Line two rimmed baking sheets with parchment paper or silicone baking mats.

7. In a stand mixer fitted with the paddle (or in a large bowl if using an electric stand mixer), beat the solidified brown butter, powdered sugar, and salt on medium-high speed, stopping to scrape down the sides of the bowl with a rubber spatula to make sure there are no butter lumps, until fluffy and lighter in color, 3 to 5 minutes.

Cookies. Make All the Cookies.

8. Add the flour and mix on low speed until combined. Stop to scrape down the bowl one last time and fold in any remaining flour streaks by hand.

9. Scoop the dough into 1½-inch balls (0.75-ounce scoop or 1½ tablespoons). Arrange on the prepared baking sheets 2 to 3 inches apart. I always arrange my cookies in five rows, alternating three across and two across—a 3-2-3-2-3 pattern—to ensure they bake evenly. Dip the tip of a finger or your thumb in water, then press a divot into the center of each cookie. Pop the pan in the fridge for 10 minutes before baking.

10. Bake the cookies in batches, rotating the pan front to back halfway through, until the cookies have lost their raw sheen and the bottoms have started to brown, 8 to 10 minutes. The cookies will remain fairly blond as they bake, so carefully lift one with a small spatula to check the bottom for doneness.

11. Allow the cookies to cool on the pan for 5 to 10 minutes before moving. When the cookies are cool enough to handle, dip the tops in powdered sugar and transfer them to a rack to finish cooling. Continue baking the remaining dough while the first batch of cookies cools.

12. Fill the well of each cookie with about ½ tablespoon pineapple jam. Store layered between parchment or waxed paper in an airtight container at room temperature for up to 2 days.

Oooh, should you start canning? That sounds like a time-consuming, labor-intensive process that requires special tools . . .

CHAI OATMEAL CREAM PIES

Makes 22 sandwich cookies

Chai and me, we're a thing. I've had one every morning for more years than I'm comfortable admitting now that I've done the math. I like my chai more spicy than sweet, which is reflected in the spice level of these cookies. Pare down the spices to just cinnamon and omit the black tea in the buttercream filling for a more classic oatmeal pie experience.

What exactly does chai mean? Why does the phrase chai tea make purists snicker?

COOKIES

2 sticks (8 ounces) unsalted butter, at room temperature

1 cup dark brown sugar

½ cup granulated sugar

1 teaspoon pure vanilla extract

1 teaspoon kosher salt

2 teaspoons ground cinnamon

½ teaspoon ground cardamom

½ teaspoon ground ginger

¼ teaspoon ground allspice

¼ teaspoon ground cloves

¼ teaspoon ground nutmeg

½ teaspoon baking soda

2 large eggs

1½ cups all-purpose flour

3 cups rolled oats

FILLING

½ cup whole milk

2 tablespoons loose black tea

8 tablespoons (4 ounces) unsalted butter, at room temperature

4 ounces vegetable shortening

2 teaspoons pure vanilla extract

⅛ teaspoon kosher salt

3½ cups powdered sugar

1. Position two oven racks in the top and bottom thirds of the oven and heat the oven to 350°F. Line two rimmed baking sheets with parchment paper or silicone baking mats.

2. Make the cookies: In a stand mixer fitted with the paddle (or in a large bowl if using an electric hand mixer), beat the butter, brown sugar, granulated sugar, vanilla, salt, cinnamon, cardamom, ginger, allspice, cloves, nutmeg, and baking soda on medium-high speed, stopping to scrape down the sides of the bowl with a rubber spatula to make sure there are no butter lumps, until light and fluffy, 3 to 5 minutes.

3. Add the eggs and mix until combined, stopping to scrape down the sides of the bowl.

4. With the mixer on low, add the flour and oats until just combined. Stop and scrape down the sides of the bowl one last time and fold in any remaining flour streaks by hand.

5. Scoop the dough into 1½-inch balls (0.75-ounce scoop or 1½ tablespoons). Arrange on the prepared baking sheets 2 to 3 inches apart in five rows, alternating three across and two across—a 3-2-3-2-3 pattern—to ensure they bake evenly.

6. Bake the cookies in batches, rotating the pan front to back halfway through, until the cookies have lost their raw sheen and started to brown along the edges, 8 to 10 minutes.

7. Allow the cookies to cool on the pan for a few minutes before moving to a rack to cool completely. Continue baking the remaining dough while the first batch of cookies cools.

8. Make the filling: In a small saucepan (or a coffee mug if using the microwave), bring the milk and black tea to a simmer over medium heat. Remove from the heat and allow the milk to steep for 20 minutes. Strain the tea out and chill the milk before adding to the buttercream.

9. In a stand mixer fitted with the paddle (or in a large bowl if using an electric hand mixer), beat the butter until smooth and no small lumps remain, 2 to 3 minutes. Scrape down the sides of the bowl and add the vegetable shortening, vanilla, and salt. Beat until the mixture is fluffy and lighter in color, stopping to scrape down the sides of the bowl, 3 to 5 minutes.

10. Turn the mixer to low speed and slowly add the powdered sugar until just combined. Stop and scrape down the sides of the bowl, then turn the mixer up to medium and beat until the filling is bright white and fluffy, 3 to 5 minutes.

11. With the mixer on low speed, add the milk 1 tablespoon at a time, until the filling reaches a spreadable consistency.

12. Spread, scoop, or pipe the buttercream onto the bottom side of half the cookies. Top each with another cookie, right side up.

13. Store layered between parchment paper, or individually wrapped in plastic wrap, in an airtight container at room temperature for up to 2 days.

50 MINUTES

Everyone loves whoopie pies, so there's never not a good time to make them! I happen to love the classic combo of chocolate and marshmallow cream filling, but they're a great vehicle for fiddling around with flavor. Roll the finished cookies in sprinkles, mini chocolate chips, or chopped nuts for a little added crunch. Or fold a few tablespoons of jam, melted chocolate, or caramel into the filling for a whole new flavor profile. It's a fun little cookie that can be reimagined in endless ways.

Why Whoopie Pie? Why not Yahoo Pie or Oh Yeah Pie? What's the deal with that name?

COOKIES

8 tablespoons (4 ounces) unsalted butter, at room temperature

1 cup granulated sugar

½ cup Dutch-process cocoa powder

1½ teaspoons baking soda

½ teaspoon kosher salt

2 large eggs

2 cups all-purpose flour

1 cup buttermilk

FILLING

10 tablespoons (5 ounces) unsalted butter, at room temperature

1 jar (7.5 ounces) marshmallow creme (like Fluff)

½ teaspoon kosher salt

1½ teaspoons pure vanilla extract

2 cups powdered sugar

1. Position two oven racks in the top and bottom thirds of the oven and heat the oven to 350°F. Line two rimmed baking sheets with parchment paper or silicone baking mats.

2. Make the cookies: In a stand mixer fitted with the paddle (or in a large bowl if using an electric hand mixer), beat the butter, granulated sugar, cocoa powder, baking soda, and salt on medium-high speed, stopping to scrape down the sides of the bowl to make sure there are no butter lumps, until fluffy and lighter in color, 3 to 5 minutes.

3. Add the eggs and mix until combined, stopping to scrape down the sides of the bowl.

4. With the mixer on low, add 1 cup of the flour until just combined. Stop and scrape down the sides of the bowl. Add the buttermilk and mix on low until combined. Scrape down the bowl again, then add the remaining 1 cup flour on low and mix until combined. Scrape down the bowl one last time and fold in any remaining flour streaks by hand.

5. Scoop the dough into 1½-inch balls (0.75-ounce scoop or 1½ tablespoons) onto the prepared baking sheets spaced 2 to 3 inches apart. These cookies will spread a little while baking. I like to arrange my cookies in five rows, alternating three across and two across—a 3-2-3-2-3 pattern—to ensure they bake evenly.

6. Bake the cookies in batches, rotating the pan front to back halfway through, until the cookies have spread, puffed up, and lost their raw sheen, 8 to 11 minutes. Continue baking the remaining dough while the first batch of cookies cools.

7. Allow the cookies to cool on the pan for a few minutes before transferring to a cooling rack.

8. Make the filling: In a stand mixer fitted with the paddle (or in a large bowl if using an electric hand mixer), beat the butter on medium-high speed, stopping to scrape down the sides of the bowl with a rubber spatula, until fluffy and no lumps remain, 3 to 5 minutes.

9. Add the marshmallow creme, salt, and vanilla and beat until combined, stopping to scrape down the sides of the bowl to make sure there are no butter lumps.

10. With the mixer on low, add the powdered sugar, 1 cup at a time, and mix until just incorporated. Stop to scrape down the bowl, then turn the mixer back up to medium-high for a minute or so to ensure it's smooth and fluffy.

11. Spread, scoop, or pipe about 2 tablespoons filling onto the bottom side of half of the cookies. Top each with another cookie right side up. If there's a spare, unmatched cookie, that's the baker's reward.

12. Store in an airtight container, or individually wrapped in plastic wrap, at room temperature for up to 3 days.

Connect the dots were my absolute favorite as a kid, probably because they offer levels of procrastination. First you kill some time carefully connecting each dot in sequence, then you get to color it in! Work on your dot-to-dot masterpiece while School Party Cupcakes (page 122) bake in the oven for the ultimate triple threat procrasti-baking experience.

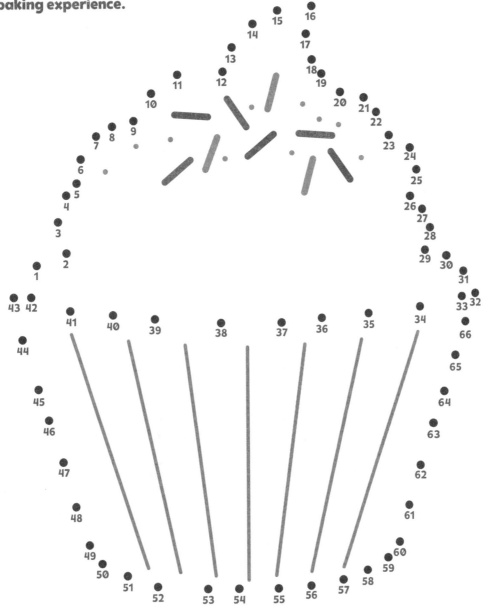

CHAPTER 5:

Late-for-Everything Loaf Cakes

iF YOU WERE A LOAF CAKE, WHAT KiND OF LOAF CAKE WOULD YOU BE?

HOW COULD I NOT INCLUDE A CHAPTER ON LOAF CAKES IN A PROCRASTIBAKING BOOK? The invitation for laziness is right in the name. Plus cake! Who doesn't love cakes? And who doesn't love cakes that masquerade as bread and infiltrate snacking opportunities all throughout the day?

ONE BANANA, TWO BANANA, THREE BANANA BREAD

20 MINUTES

Sometimes you have three overripe bananas, sometimes you have one. This recipe is at your service, no matter how much or how little you've ignored your produce. Each quantity doubles the volume of batter, so your baking vessel will change with each batch. If you ever want to make a larger batch, but only have ripe bananas, throw them onto a baking sheet (peel and all) and roast in a 300°F oven for 10 to 15 minutes to soften.

MAKES:

1 MINI LOAF	2 MINI LOAVES OR 1 SHORT STANDARD LOAF	1 STANDARD LOAF
½ cup all-purpose flour	1 cup all-purpose flour	1½ cups all-purpose flour
½ teaspoon ground cinnamon	1 teaspoon ground cinnamon	1½ teaspoons ground cinnamon
½ teaspoon baking soda	1 teaspoon baking soda	1½ teaspoons baking soda
¼ teaspoon baking powder	½ teaspoon baking powder	1 teaspoon baking powder
¼ teaspoon kosher salt	½ teaspoon kosher salt	1 teaspoon kosher salt
1 ripe banana	2 ripe bananas	3 ripe bananas
⅓ cup dark brown sugar	⅔ cup dark brown sugar	1 cup dark brown sugar
1 large egg	2 large eggs	3 large eggs
¾ teaspoon pure vanilla extract	1½ teaspoons pure vanilla extract	2¼ teaspoons pure vanilla extract
4 tablespoons (2 ounces) unsalted butter, melted	8 tablespoons (4 ounces) unsalted butter, melted	12 tablespoons (6 ounces) unsalted butter, melted
1 tablespoon vegetable oil	2 tablespoons vegetable oil	3 tablespoons vegetable oil
Turbinado sugar, for sprinkling on top	Turbinado sugar, for sprinkling on top	Turbinado sugar, for sprinkling on top

Late-for-Everything Loaf Cakes

1. Position a rack in the center of the oven and heat the oven to 325°F. Cut parchment paper to line the bottom(s) of your chosen loaf pan(s). Grease the bottom(s) of your chosen pan(s) before adding paper to help it stick. Grease the paper and sides of the pan(s) and flour them.

2. In a large bowl, whisk together the flour, cinnamon, baking soda, baking powder, and salt.

3. In a stand mixer fitted with the paddle (or in a large bowl if using an electric hand mixer), beat the banana(s) and brown sugar on medium-high speed until the banana is pulverized and liquefied, 3 to 5 minutes. Stop and scrape down the sides of the bowl to make sure there are no banana chunks.

4. Take the bowl off the mixer and whisk in the egg(s) by hand, one at a time.

5. Whisk in the vanilla, melted butter, and oil until combined.

6. Pour the wet ingredients into the dry and fold until just combined. Pour the batter into the prepared baking pan and spread it level.

7. Bake, rotating the pan halfway through, until a toothpick inserted in the middle comes out clean or with a few crumbs clinging to it, 15 to 20 minutes for the mini loaves and 25 to 30 minutes for the standard loaf.

8. Transfer the pan to a rack to cool until it's cool enough to handle, 15 to 20 minutes. Carefully turn the bread out of the pan and set on a rack to cool completely before storing. Store wrapped in plastic wrap or in an airtight container at room temperature for up to 3 days.

GINGERBREAD

20 MINUTES

Makes 1 loaf

There's so much flavor packed into this extremely tender cake that there's no need to top it with anything creamy or crunchy. If you feel inclined to guild the lily, cream cheese frosting pairs beautifully, as does a scoop of vanilla ice cream.

4 tablespoons (2 ounces) unsalted butter, at room temperature

½ cup dark brown sugar

2 teaspoons ground cinnamon

1½ teaspoons baking powder

1½ teaspoons ground ginger

½ teaspoon kosher salt

¼ teaspoon ground allspice

¼ teaspoon ground nutmeg

⅛ teaspoon ground cardamom

Pinch of white pepper

3 large eggs

½ cup molasses

¾ cup warm water

½ teaspoon baking soda

1¼ cups all-purpose flour

1. Position a rack in the center of the oven and heat the oven to 325°F. Cut a piece of parchment paper to line the bottom of an 8½ x 4½ x 2¾-inch loaf pan. Grease the bottom of the pan before adding the paper to help it stick. Grease the paper and sides of the pan and flour them.

2. In a stand mixer fitted with the paddle (or in a large bowl if using an electric hand mixer), beat the butter, brown sugar, cinnamon, baking powder, ginger, salt, allspice, nutmeg, cardamom, and white pepper on medium-high speed, stopping to scrape down the sides of the bowl with a rubber spatula to make sure there are no butter lumps, until fluffy and lighter in color, 3 to 5 minutes.

3. Add the eggs, one at at time, and mix until combined, stopping to scrape down the sides of the bowl.

4. In a small bowl or glass measuring cup, whisk together the molasses, water, and baking soda.

5. With the mixer on low, slowly add the flour and mix until combined. Stop and scrape down the sides of the bowl, then turn the mixer back on low. Slowly add the molasses mixture and mix until combined. Stop to scrape down the sides of the bowl one last time to make sure all the ingredients are well incorporated. Pour the batter into the prepared pan and spread it level.

6. Bake, rotating the pan front to back halfway through, until a toothpick inserted in the center comes out clean or with a few crumbs clinging to it, 40 to 45 minutes.

7. Allow the cake to cool in the pan until it's cool enough to handle. Turn out onto a platter or cutting board.

8. Store wrapped or in an airtight container at room temperature for up to 3 days.

Late-for-Everything Loaf Cakes

PUMPKIN SPICE BREAD
Makes 1 loaf

Calling all my basic chicks—your bread is ready! Pumpkin spice has become totally cliché, but who cares? It's delicious! Put it in your coffee, your deodorant, your dryer sheets, your car oil—anything goes! This bread sees you and celebrates you in all your pumpkin spice–loving ways.

Why settle for simple toasted nuts when you could top your Pumpkin Bread with the candied pecans from the Turtle Layer Cake (page 186)?

PUMPKIN SPICE BREAD

1½ cups cake flour

1 teaspoon baking powder

½ teaspoon baking soda

¾ teaspoon ground cinnamon

½ teaspoon ground ginger

½ teaspoon kosher salt

⅛ teaspoon ground allspice

⅛ teaspoon ground cloves

1 cup granulated sugar

1 can (7-ounces) unsweetened pumpkin puree (about 1 cup)

½ cup vegetable oil

1 teaspoon pure vanilla extract

2 large eggs

FROSTING

8 tablespoons (4 ounces) unsalted butter, at room temperature

4 ounces cream cheese, at room temperature

1 teaspoon pure vanilla extract

1½ cups powdered sugar

½ teaspoon ground cinnamon

½ cup chopped toasted pecans or walnuts (optional)

1. Position a rack in the center of the oven and heat the oven to 325°F. Cut a piece of parchment paper to line the bottom of an 8½ x 4½ x 2¾-inch loaf pan. Grease the bottom of the pan before adding the paper to help it stick. Grease the paper and sides of the pan and flour them.

2. Make the pumpkin spice bread: In a large bowl, whisk together the cake flour, baking powder, baking soda, cinnamon, ginger, salt, allspice, and cloves.

3. In a separate medium bowl or large glass measuring cup, whisk together the granulated sugar, pumpkin, oil, and vanilla until combined. Whisk in the eggs.

4. Pour the wet mixture into the dry ingredients and whisk until combined. When the batter becomes too thick to whisk, switch to a rubber spatula. Stir until the flour is completely incorporated. Pour the batter into the prepared pan and spread it level.

5. Bake, rotating the pan front to back halfway through, until a toothpick inserted in the center of the cake comes out clean or with a few crumbs clinging to it, 45 to 50 minutes.

6. Transfer the cake to a rack to cool in the pan until the pan is cool enough to handle. Carefully turn the loaf out and return it to the rack. Allow the cake to cool completely before frosting or storing. The unfrosted cake can be stored wrapped at room temperature overnight, or up to 3 days in the fridge.

7. Make the frosting: In a stand mixer fitted with the paddle (or in a large bowl if using an electric hand mixer), beat the butter on medium-high speed until it's light and fluffy, about 5 minutes. Stop to scrape down the sides of the bowl to ensure all the butter gets creamed.

8. On medium speed, add the cream cheese and vanilla until just combined, about 3 minutes more.

9. Turn the mixer to low speed and add the powdered sugar and cinnamon, about ½ cup at a time, and mix until incorporated.

10. Spread the frosting over the top of the pumpkin loaf and finish with a sprinkling of the toasted nuts (if using).

11. Store the cake, covered, at room temperature for up to 8 hours, and in the fridge overnight or up to 3 days.

Most canned pumpkin puree isn't actually pumpkin. What exactly is it?

40 MINUTES

ZUCCHINI-LIME BREAD
Makes 1 loaf

This is the perfect thing to make when you want to pretend that you're making something good for you. I mean, it's not *terrible* for you. How could anything with ¾ cup of zucchini in it be terrible for you? Most versions of this bread get all spicy with cinnamon and ginger added in, but I prefer to head in a different flavor direction, brightening things up with a little citrus. Lemon will do if you don't have a lime on hand.

2½ cups all-purpose flour

½ teaspoon baking powder

½ teaspoon baking soda

1 teaspoon kosher salt

4 large eggs

1 cup granulated sugar

¾ cup vegetable oil

¼ cup sour cream

2 teaspoons grated lime zest (about 1 large)

1 teaspoon pure vanilla extract

1½ cups shredded zucchini, drained (about 1 large or 2 small)

2 tablespoons turbinado sugar, for sprinkling

1. Position a rack in the center of the oven and heat the oven to 325°F. Cut a piece of parchment paper to line the bottom of an 8½ x 4½ x 2¾-inch loaf pan. Grease the bottom of the pan before adding the paper to help it stick. Grease the paper and sides of the pan and flour them.

2. In a large bowl, whisk together the flour, baking powder, baking soda, and salt.

3. In a separate medium bowl or large glass measuring cup, whisk together the eggs, granulated sugar, oil, sour cream, lime zest, and vanilla.

4. Pour the wet mixture into the dry ingredients and stir until combined. Fold in the shredded zucchini. Pour the batter into the prepared pan, spread it level, and sprinkle the turbinado sugar over the top.

5. Bake, rotating the pan front to back halfway through, until a toothpick inserted in the center of the cake comes out clean or with a few crumbs clinging to it, 1 hour to 1 hour 10 minutes.

6. Allow the cake to cool in the pan until it is cool enough to handle. Carefully turn the loaf out onto a cutting board or platter.

7. Store wrapped or in an airtight container at room temperature for up to 3 days.

BLUEBERRY BUCKLE
Makes 1 loaf

This cake will change your mind about baked fruit. Well, if you're already into baked fruit, this will reaffirm your feelings. If you're not, then this could bring you over to the fruity side. It's basically just enough of a soft biscuit dough to hold together an impossible amount of fresh blueberries, topped with a crunchy streusel. Use the best, in-season blueberries you can find since the fruit is the star of the show. This cake is the perfect weekend breakfast or a decadent summery snack.

STREUSEL

- ½ cup all-purpose flour
- ½ cup rolled oats
- 2 tablespoons granulated sugar
- ½ teaspoon ground cinnamon
- ½ teaspoon kosher salt
- 4 tablespoons (2 ounces) unsalted butter, at room temperature

CAKE

- 10 tablespoons (5 ounces) unsalted butter, at room temperature
- ⅔ cup granulated sugar
- ½ teaspoon kosher salt
- Grated zest of 1 lemon
- 1½ tablespoons pure vanilla extract
- 1½ tablespoons baking powder
- 2 large eggs
- 1½ cups all-purpose flour
- 4 cups fresh blueberries

1. Position a rack in the center of the oven and heat the oven to 325°F. Cut a piece of parchment paper to line the bottom of an 8½ x 4½ x 2¾-inch loaf pan. Grease the bottom of the pan before adding the paper to help it stick. Grease the paper and sides of the pan and flour them.

2. Make the streusel: In a large bowl, combine the flour, oats, sugar, cinnamon, salt, and butter. Pinch and toss the butter into the dry ingredients to combine until it has a sandy consistency.

3. Make the cake: In a stand mixer fitted with the paddle (or a large bowl if using an electric stand mixer), beat together the butter, sugar, salt, lemon zest, vanilla, and baking powder on medium-high speed until fluffy and lighter in color, stopping to scrape down the sides of the bowl with a rubber spatula to make sure there are no butter lumps, 3 to 5 minutes.

4. Add the eggs, one at a time, until completely combined. Stop and scrape down the sides of the bowl halfway through mixing and after adding the last egg.

5. With the mixer on low, slowly add the flour to the butter mixture until just incorporated. Scrape down the sides of the bowl one last time.

6. Add the blueberries and carefully fold them into the batter by hand. When I say by hand, I mean use your freshly washed hands to gently fold the large amount of blueberries into the much smaller amount of batter. Do your best to prevent breaking the blueberries. It's inevitable that a few will pop—just try not to turn your batter blue. Carefully transfer the batter to the prepared pan and top with the streusel.

7. Bake, rotating the pan front to back halfway through, until a toothpick inserted into a cakier part comes out clean or with a few crumbs clinging to it, about 1 hour. This cake can be tricky to check for doneness because of all the fruit. The topping and edges will be golden brown and the cake should spring back to the touch.

8. Transfer the pan to a rack to cool for at least 20 minutes. The loaf would fall apart if you tried to remove it too soon. Once the pan is cool enough to handle, carefully turn the loaf out onto a plate or cutting board instead of a cooling rack. You want to avoid having to move it too many times to prevent breakage. Sprinkle any crumble that falls off in the process back onto the top of the cake.

9. Buckle is best enjoyed shortly after baking, but can be stored, wrapped, in the fridge for up to 2 days. Gently warm the leftover cake covered in a low oven before serving.

What's a buckle? Did you make that up or is that a real thing?

This cake is the ideal excuse for a trip to your local PYO farm since only fresh blueberries will do.

ORANGE MARMALADE BREAD

Makes 1 loaf

I struggled to choose which version of this bread to include, because the recipe works with any chunky-style jam or marmalade. Ginger preserves, peach preserves, and orange-cherry marmalade are all fun ones to try. Use what you have on hand to create your own unique loaf cake.

CAKE

- 1½ sticks (6 ounces) unsalted butter, at room temperature
- ½ cup granulated sugar
- ½ cup orange marmalade
- 2 tablespoons fresh orange juice
- 1 teaspoon baking powder
- ½ teaspoon kosher salt
- 1 teaspoon pure vanilla extract
- 2 large eggs
- 1½ cups all-purpose flour
- ½ cup whole milk

GLAZE

- ½ cup powdered sugar
- 1½ tablespoons fresh orange juice
- Orange zest, for garnish (optional)

1. Position a rack in the center of the oven and heat the oven to 325°F. Cut a piece of parchment paper to line the bottom of an 8½ x 4½ x 2¾-inch loaf pan. Grease the bottom of the pan before adding the paper to help it stick. Grease the paper and sides of the pan and flour them.

2. Make the cake: In a stand mixer fitted with the paddle (or in a large bowl if using an electric hand mixer), beat together the butter, granulated sugar, marmalade, orange juice, baking powder, salt, and vanilla at medium speed until fluffy and lighter in color, stopping to scrape down the sides of the bowl with a rubber spatula to make sure there are no butter lumps, 3 to 5 minutes.

3. Add the eggs, one at a time, until completely combined. Stop and scrape down the sides of the bowl halfway through mixing and after adding the last egg.

4. With the mixer on low, add half of the flour to the butter mixture until just incorporated. Slowly add half of the milk until combined. Stop and scrape down the sides of the bowl. Add the remaining flour and mix until just incorporated. Add the last of the milk and mix until just combined. Pour the batter into the prepared pan and spread it level.

5. Bake, rotating the pan front to back halfway through, until a toothpick inserted in the center comes out clean or with a few crumbs clinging to it, 40 to 45 minutes.

6. Transfer the cake to a rack to cool in the pan until cool enough to handle. Carefully turn the loaf out and return it to the rack.

7. Make the glaze: In a small bowl, whisk together the powdered sugar and orange juice until combined.

8. Spoon the glaze over the top of the warm cake. Sprinkle with orange zest to garnish.

9. Store covered or in an airtight container at room temperature for up to 3 days.

What's the difference between marmalade and jam? What about jelly?

RASPBERRY-HIBISCUS LOAF CAKE
Makes 1 loaf

This loaf cake recipe was created as a tribute to my standing Starbucks treat-yo'self-at-3-p.m. order: venti iced passion tea lemonade, unsweetened, with a slice of lemon loaf. With this recipe, I've combined the flavors of that standing order to create an aromatic cake perfect for nibbling with a cup of tea or slicing up for brunch. Buy freeze-dried raspberry powder or make your own by using a rolling pin to smash freeze-dried raspberries in a zip-top bag.

CAKE

1 cup whole milk

2 Tazo passion tea bags (or your favorite brand of hibiscus tea)

¼ cup freeze-dried raspberry powder

1½ cups cake flour

1 teaspoon baking powder

½ teaspoon baking soda

½ teaspoon kosher salt

6 tablespoons vegetable oil

1 cup granulated sugar

¾ teaspoon pure vanilla extract

2 tablespoons lemon juice

2 large eggs

GLAZE

1 cup powdered sugar

2 tablespoons lemon juice

1 teaspoon whole milk

Lemon zest, for garnish (optional)

1. Make the cake: In a small saucepan (or a coffee mug if using the microwave), scald the milk and tea bags. Remove from the heat, cover, and allow the tea to steep for 20 minutes. Remove the tea bags and wring them out into the pan to remove any milk they've absorbed. Discard the tea bags.

2. Position a rack in the center of the oven and heat the oven to 325°F. Cut a piece of parchment paper to line the bottom of an 8½ x 4½ x 2¾-inch loaf pan. Grease the bottom of the pan before adding the paper to help it stick. Grease the paper and sides of the pan and flour them.

3. In a large bowl, whisk together the freeze-dried raspberry powder, cake flour, baking powder, baking soda, and salt.

4. In a small bowl or large glass measuring cup, whisk together the oil, granulated sugar, vanilla, lemon juice, and hibiscus milk until combined. Add the eggs and whisk until combined.

5. Add the dry ingredients to the wet and fold to combine. Pour the batter into the prepared pan and spread it level.

6. Bake, rotating the pan front to back halfway through, until a toothpick inserted in the center of the cake comes out clean or with a few crumbs clinging to it, 45 to 50 minutes.

7. Transfer the cake to a rack to cool in the pan until the pan is cool enough to handle. Carefully turn the loaf out and return it to the rack. Allow the cake to cool completely before glazing or storing. The unglazed cake can be stored wrapped at room temperature overnight, or up to 3 days in the fridge.

8. Make the glaze: In a small bowl, whisk together the powdered sugar, lemon juice, and milk until combined.

9. Spoon the glaze over the top of the warm cake. Sprinkle with lemon zest to garnish. Store, covered, at room temperature for up to 3 days.

Late-for-Everything Loaf Cakes

BLACK-AND-WHITE LOAF CAKE
Makes 1 loaf

This loaf cake is like a black and white cookie supersized and turned inside out. Creating the split-down-the-middle illusion is simple but showstopping. You'll get oohs and aahs at your next brunch or just be very happy with yourself during your next snack break. Baking the loaf longer and at a lower temperature helps to ensure a tender cake with edges that are not too browned.

Who was the genius to design the iconic black-and-white cookie? And why'd they do it?

CAKE

1½ sticks (6 ounces) unsalted butter, at room temperature

½ teaspoon kosher salt

½ teaspoon baking soda

1 cup granulated sugar

1 teaspoon pure vanilla extract

4 ounces cream cheese, at room temperature

3 large eggs

1½ cups all-purpose flour

¼ cup Dutch-process cocoa powder

GLAZE

1 cup powdered sugar

2 tablespoons whole milk

1 teaspoon pure vanilla extract

1. Position a rack in the center of the oven and heat the oven to 325°F. Cut a piece of parchment paper to line the bottom of an 8½ x 4½ x 2¾-inch loaf pan. Grease the bottom of the pan before adding the paper to help it stick. Grease the paper and sides of the pan and flour them.

2. Make the cake: In a stand mixer fitted with the paddle (or in a large bowl if using an electric hand mixer), beat the butter, salt, baking soda, granulated sugar, and vanilla at medium speed until well incorporated and lighter in color, stopping to scrape down the sides of the bowl to make sure there are no butter lumps, 3 to 5 minutes.

3. Add the cream cheese and mix until combined. Scrape down the sides of the bowl, then add the eggs, one at a time. Stop and scrape down the sides of the bowl after the last egg.

4. With the mixer on low, slowly add the flour to the butter mixture until just incorporated. Scrape down the sides of the bowl one last time. Fold in any remaining streaks of flour by hand.

5. Pour half of the batter into a small bowl and fold in the cocoa powder.

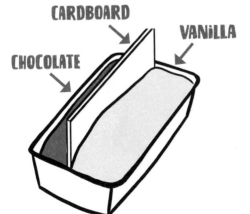

CARDBOARD

VANILLA

CHOCOLATE

6. Cut a piece of cardboard 8½ inches long and at least 4 inches high. (A pizza box or extra cake board both work great.) Wrap the piece of cardboard with plastic wrap and grease both sides. Position the cardboard divider down the center of the pan lengthwise. This is a great time to employ a second set of hands to hold the cardboard while you pour. If you're doing this solo, place a measuring cup on its side in the empty half of the pan to prop up the board. Pour the vanilla batter into one side of the pan and the chocolate into the other. Carefully and slowly pull the cardboard divider out of the batter, wiggling the board a little as you go to release any batter that sticks to it. Once you've removed the divider, gently tap the pan against your work surface to bring the two batters together and smooth the top.

7. Bake, rotating the pan front to back halfway through, until a toothpick inserted in the center of the cake comes out clean or with a few crumbs clinging to it, 1 hour to 1 hour 20 minutes.

8. Transfer the pan to a rack to cool for at least 20 minutes or until the pan is cool enough to handle. Carefully turn the cake out and return it to the rack to cool completely, at least 1 hour, before icing.

9. Make the glaze: In a small bowl, whisk together the powdered sugar, milk, and vanilla.

10. Spread the icing over the top of the cooled cake with a butter knife or an offset spatula. Serve immediately or store, wrapped, at room temperature for up to 3 days. Allow the icing to firm up before storing, about 30 minutes.

PINEAPPLE UPSIDE-DOWN LOAF
Makes 1 loaf

When I was growing up, the pineapple upside-down cake I knew was baked in a sheet cake pan with our finest yellow cake boxed mix. In my grown-up version, I pair a sturdier (homemade) honey pound cake with the classic sweet-tart pineapple-cherry-caramel topping. Baking this cake in a loaf pan also provides for what I feel is a more balanced cake-to-fruit ratio. My preferred pan to bake this cake in is a small Pullman loaf pan because it's long and narrow, but it will work just fine in a standard loaf pan as well.

TOPPING

4 tablespoons (2 ounces) unsalted butter

⅓ cup dark brown sugar

3 pineapple slices, ¼-inch thick and core removed (fresh or canned)

6 maraschino cherries (or pitted fresh cherries)

CAKE

1½ sticks (6 ounces) unsalted butter, at room temperature

½ cup granulated sugar

½ cup honey

1 teaspoon baking powder

½ teaspoon kosher salt

1 teaspoon pure vanilla extract

2 large eggs

1½ cups all-purpose flour

½ cup whole milk

1. Position a rack in the center of the oven and heat the oven to 325°F.

2. Make the topping: Drop 2 ounces of the butter into a 9 x 4-inch loaf pan (or regular loaf pan if you don't have a Pullman) and place it in the oven to melt the butter. Remove the pan from the oven and sprinkle the brown sugar over the melted butter. Cut the pineapple slices in half down through the middle where the core was to create little crescent shapes. Line the half-moons up in the bottom of the pan all facing the same direction. (See the Late for Everything Loaf Cakes picture in the photo insert.) Place a cherry in each of the small openings (where the core once was). Trim the cherries to fit if needed. Grease the sides of the pan and set it aside.

3. Make the cake: In a stand mixer fitted with the paddle (or in a large bowl if using an electric hand mixer), beat together the butter, granulated sugar, honey, baking powder, salt, and vanilla at medium speed until fluffy and lighter in color, stopping to scrape down the sides of the bowl with a rubber spatula to make sure there are no butter lumps, 3 to 5 minutes.

4. Add the eggs, one at a time, until completely combined. Stop and scrape down the sides of the bowl halfway through mixing and after adding the last egg.

5. With the mixer on low, add half of the flour to the butter mixture until just incorporated. Slowly add half of the milk until combined. Stop and scrape down the sides of the bowl. Add the remaining flour and mix until just incorporated. Add the last of the milk and mix until just combined.

6. Carefully pour the batter into the prepared pan over the cherries and pineapple slices and spread it level.

7. Bake, rotating the pan front to back halfway through, until a toothpick inserted in the center of the cake comes out clean or with a few crumbs clinging to it, 50 to 55 minutes.

8. Transfer the cake to a rack to cool in the pan until the pan is cool enough to handle. Run a butter knife or an offset spatula around the outside of the cake, making sure the knife hits the bottom of the pan as you go. Carefully turn the cake out onto a cutting board. Set it on its side and trim the domed part of the cake if it's not sitting flat enough for you. Return the cake to the rack to cool or transfer it to a serving platter. The cake is best enjoyed the day it's baked, but can be stored, covered, at room temperature for up to 3 days.

Fancy up your finished cake with a drizzle of the caramel sauce from the Turtle Layer Cake recipe (page 186).

Late-for-Everything Loaf Cakes

CHAPTER 6:

Fear-of-Success Snack Cakes

iF YOU WERE A CUPCAKE, WHAT KiND OF CUPCAKE WOULD YOU BE?

SNACKING, WHEN DONE APPROPRIATELY, EXISTS TO FUEL US THROUGH OUR HECTIC, MODERN DAYS FULL OF NEVER-ENDING TASKS. It also exists as something to do while binge-watching makeup tutorials in one tab while you keep your work-related tabs open at the bottom of the screen glaring at you, staring deep into your soul, wondering when you'll decide it's time to pretend to be a productive member of society again. Or something. Snack cakes are here to serve you on both accounts! Sweet treats to pep up the laggy part of your day and delicious distractions for the rest.

OLIVE OIL APPLE SNACK CAKE

Makes 18 to 24 servings

The addition of olive oil gives this cake a complex, subtle floral flavor and helps keep the cake tender into day three. I will sometimes add a crumble to the top before baking or a dollop of cream cheese frosting after it's baked, but honestly, it's not necessary. This is a perfect little snack cake for brunch or anytime the munchies roll around.

3 large eggs

1½ cups granulated sugar

1 cup extra-virgin olive oil

2 teaspoons pure vanilla extract

1 cup sour cream

2 cups all-purpose flour

1 teaspoon kosher salt

1 teaspoon baking soda

1 teaspoon ground cinnamon

½ teaspoon ground allspice

½ teaspoon ground cloves

½ teaspoon white pepper

2 cups diced peeled apples

1. Position a rack in the center of the oven and heat the oven to 325°F. Grease and flour a 13 x 9-inch baking pan.

2. In a large bowl, whisk together the eggs and sugar until fluffy and lighter in color, 2 to 3 minutes.

3. Whisk in the oil, vanilla, and sour cream to combine.

4. In a smaller bowl, whisk together the flour, salt, baking soda, cinnamon, allspice, cloves, and white pepper.

5. Add the dry ingredients to the wet and fold to combine. When a few flour streaks remain, add the apples and fold to combine. Pour the batter into the prepared pan and spread it level.

6. Bake, rotating the pan front to back halfway through, until a toothpick inserted in the center comes out clean or with a few crumbs clinging to it, 25 to 30 minutes.

7. Transfer the pan to a rack to cool. When the pan is cool enough to handle, carefully turn the cake out onto a plate or cutting board or keep the cake in the pan and serve from there. Cut the cake into 18 large or 24 smaller pieces. Or sneakily pick away at it like little mice, one sliver at a time.

8. Store the cake, covered, at room temperature for up to 3 days.

Make the crumble topping from the **Cheesecake-Stuffed Nutella Coffee Cake (page 130)** and sprinkle it over the batter (step 5) before baking.

40 MINUTES

GOLDEN BANANA CAKE
Makes 18 to 24 servings

This bright and yummy cake is a celebration of banana flavor with none of the cinnamon or brown sugar to get in the way. The tart and tangy buttermilk frosting perfectly balances with the banana's sweetness. I would have no shame serving this cake for breakfast, brunch, or in the afternoon with a cup of tea.

CAKE

3 sticks (12 ounces) unsalted butter, at room temperature

1⅓ cups granulated sugar

¾ teaspoon baking soda

½ teaspoon baking powder

½ teaspoon kosher salt

1 tablespoon pure vanilla extract

6 large eggs

1 cup mashed banana

¼ cup buttermilk

2¼ cups cake flour

BUTTERMILK FROSTING

2 sticks (8 ounces) unsalted butter, at room temperature

4 cups powdered sugar

1 tablespoon pure vanilla extract

¼ teaspoon kosher salt

3 tablespoons buttermilk

1. Position a rack in the center of the oven and heat the oven to 350°F. Grease and flour a 13 x 9-inch baking dish.

2. Make the cake: In a stand mixer fitted with the paddle (or in a medium bowl if using an electric hand mixer), beat the butter, granulated sugar, baking soda, baking powder, salt, and vanilla on medium-high speed until light and fluffy, 3 minutes or so, stopping occasionally to scrape down the sides of the bowl with a rubber spatula.

3. Add the eggs, one at a time, and mix until combined, stopping to scrape down the sides of the bowl halfway through and after the last egg.

4. In a small bowl or large glass measuring cup, whisk together the mashed banana and buttermilk.

5. With the mixer on low speed, add the banana/buttermilk mixture until combined.

6. Add the flour and mix on low until just incorporated. Stop to scrape down the sides of the bowl one last time. Fold in any remaining flour streaks by hand.

7. Pour the batter into the prepared pan and spread it level.

8. Bake, rotating the pan front to back halfway through, until a toothpick inserted in the center of the cake comes out clean or with a few crumbs clinging to it, 25 to 30 minutes.

9. Transfer the dish to a rack to cool. Allow the cake to cool completely before frosting. Turn the cake out onto a platter or leave it in the dish for serving.

10. Make the frosting: In a stand mixer fitted with the paddle (or in a large bowl if using an electric hand mixer), beat the butter and powdered sugar on medium speed until light and fluffy, stopping occasionally to scrape down the sides of the bowl with a rubber spatula to make sure there are no butter lumps, 3 to 5 minutes.

11. With the mixer on low, add the vanilla, salt, and buttermilk until just combined. Stop and scrape down the sides of the bowl one last time.

12. Spread the frosting over the cooled cake with an offset spatula or the back of a spoon. Cut into 18 large or 24 smaller pieces. Store covered at room temperature for up to 8 hours, and in the fridge for up to 3 days.

Fear-of-Success Snack Cakes

40 MINUTES

CHOCOLATE CHIP SNACK CAKE
Makes 24 servings

This is the perfect snack cake when you just want a sliver, not a hunk. It's thin, like a bar cookie, but satisfying when the craving calls for cake. My kids love chocolate chips in anything, but if it's different in your house, omit them or swap in your favorite baking chip or sprinkles.

CAKE

3 cups cake flour

½ cup mini chocolate chips

1½ teaspoons baking powder

½ teaspoon baking soda

1 teaspoon kosher salt

1½ cups buttermilk

1½ cups granulated sugar

¾ cup vegetable oil

4 large eggs

1 tablespoon pure vanilla extract

FROSTING

8 tablespoons (4 ounces) unsalted butter, at room temperature

4 ounces vegetable shortening (or more butter)

2 teaspoons pure vanilla extract

⅛ teaspoon kosher salt

3½ cups powdered sugar

2 to 4 tablespoons whole milk

½ cup mini chocolate chips, for garnish

1. Position a rack in the center of the oven and heat the oven to 325°F. Line a rimmed baking sheet with parchment paper. Grease the sheet before placing the paper to prevent it from sliding around. Grease and flour the paper and sides of the pan.

2. Make the cake: In a large bowl, whisk together the cake flour, chocolate chips, baking powder, baking soda, and salt.

3. In a smaller bowl or large glass measuring cup, whisk together the buttermilk, granulated sugar, oil, eggs, and vanilla.

4. Add the wet ingredients to the dry and fold to combine.

5. Pour the batter into the prepared pan and spread it level.

6. Bake, rotating the pan front to back halfway through, or until a toothpick inserted into the middle of the cake comes out clean or with a few crumbs clinging to it, 15 to 18 minutes.

7. Transfer the pan to a rack to cool completely before frosting.

8. Make the frosting: In a stand mixer fitted with the paddle (or in a large bowl if using an electric hand mixer), beat the butter on medium-high speed until smooth and no small lumps remain, 2 to 3 minutes. Scrape down the sides of the bowl and add the vegetable shortening, vanilla, and salt. Beat until the mixture is fluffy and lighter in color, stopping to scrape down the sides of the bowl, 3 to 5 minutes.

9. Turn the mixer to low speed and slowly add the powdered sugar until just combined. Stop and scrape down the sides of the bowl, then turn the mixer up to medium and beat until the frosting is bright white and fluffy, 3 to 5 minutes.

10. With the mixer on low speed, add the milk 1 tablespoon at a time, until a spreadable frosting consistency is achieved.

11. Spread the frosting over the cake and sprinkle with chocolate chips.

12. Store covered or in an airtight container for up to 8 hours, and in the fridge for up to 3 days.

STRAWBERRY-BANANA CAKE
Makes 18 to 24 servings

You could eat this cake for breakfast. You're a grown-up, so you can eat anything for breakfast. This cake in particular is amazing in the morning with your caffeinator of choice. It's also a top-notch way to use up fruit that's past its prime. If you've got more bananas and less strawberries or vice versa, don't sweat it. As long as your pureed fruit doesn't exceed one cup or so, the cake will still be stellar.

Why do fresh bananas and banana-flavored things taste so different?

CAKE

5 ounces strawberries (about 8 large)

1 medium banana

1½ cups vegetable oil

1 tablespoon lemon juice

2¼ cups cake flour

1½ teaspoons baking powder

¾ teaspoon baking soda

1 teaspoon kosher salt

3 large eggs

1 cup granulated sugar

1 teaspoon pure vanilla extract

CREAM CHEESE FROSTING

2 sticks (8 ounces) unsalted butter, at room temperature

8 ounces cream cheese, at room temperature

1½ teaspoons pure vanilla extract

3½ cups powdered sugar

Sprinkles or sliced fruit, for garnish

1. Position a rack in the center of the oven and heat the oven to 350°F. Grease and flour a 13 x 9-inch baking dish or pan.

2. Make the cake: In a blender, combine the strawberries, banana, oil, and lemon juice and pulse to puree.

3. In a large bowl, whisk together the cake flour, baking powder, baking soda, and salt.

4. In a separate small bowl or large glass measuring cup, whisk together the fruit puree, eggs, granulated sugar, and vanilla.

5. Pour the wet mixture into the dry and whisk until combined. When the batter becomes too thick to whisk, switch to a rubber spatula. Stir until the flour is just incorporated, then pour the batter into the prepared baking dish and spread it level.

6. Bake, rotating the pan front to back halfway through, until a toothpick inserted in the center comes out clean or with a few crumbs clinging to it, 25 to 30 minutes.

7. Transfer the pan to a rack to cool. Allow the cake to cool completely before frosting. Turn the cake out onto a platter or leave it in the dish and serve from there.

8. Make the cream cheese frosting: In a stand mixer fitted with the paddle (or in a large bowl if using an electric hand mixer), beat the butter on medium-high speed until it's light and fluffy, about 5 minutes. Stop to scrape down the sides of the bowl to ensure all the butter gets creamed.

9. On medium speed, beat in the cream cheese and vanilla until just combined, about 3 minutes more.

10. Turn the mixer to low speed and add the powdered sugar, about 1 cup at a time, and mix until incorporated.

11. Spread the frosting over the cooled cake using an offset spatula or the back of a spoon. Top with sprinkles or fresh fruit. Cut into 18 large or 24 smaller pieces.

12. Store wrapped or in an airtight container at room temperature for up to 8 hours, and in the fridge for up to 3 days.

BLACKBERRY-CASHEW SHEET CAKE
Makes 18 to 24 servings

The flavor combo of this cake and frosting is like a fancy-pants PB&J. If you don't happen to have cashew butter on hand, swap in whatever nut or seed butter you have in your pantry. Same goes for the jam. Use whatever's your jam.

CAKE

1½ sticks (6 ounces) unsalted butter, at room temperature

¾ cup (6 ounces) cashew butter

¾ cup granulated sugar

1 teaspoon pure vanilla extract

1½ teaspoons baking powder

1 teaspoon kosher salt

5 large eggs

¾ cup cake flour

BLACKBERRY SWIRLED CREAM CHEESE FROSTING

2 sticks (8 ounces) unsalted butter, at room temperature

8 ounces cream cheese, at room temperature

1½ teaspoons pure vanilla extract

3½ cups powdered sugar

½ cup blackberry jam

1. Position a rack in the center of the oven and heat the oven to 350°F. Grease and flour a 13 x 9-inch baking dish.

2. Make the cake: In a stand mixer fitted with the paddle (or in a large bowl if using an electric hand mixer), beat together the butter, cashew butter, granulated sugar, vanilla, baking powder, and salt at medium speed until well incorporated and lighter in color, stopping to scrape down the sides of the bowl with a rubber spatula to make sure there are no butter lumps, 3 to 5 minutes.

3. Add the eggs, one at a time, until completely combined. Stop and scrape down the sides of the bowl halfway through mixing and after adding the last egg.

4. With the mixer on low, slowly add the cake flour to the butter mixture until just incorporated. Scrape down the sides of the bowl one last time. Fold in any remaining streaks of flour by hand. Pour the batter into the prepared baking dish and spread it level.

5. Bake, rotating the pan front to back halfway through, until a toothpick inserted in the center of the cake comes out clean or with a few crumbs clinging to it, 25 to 30 minutes.

6. Allow the cake to cool completely in the pan on a cooling rack before frosting or storing. Store the cake wrapped at room temperature overnight or in the fridge for up to 3 days.

7. Make the blackberry swirled cream cheese frosting: In a stand mixer fitted with the paddle (or in a large bowl if using an electric hand mixer), beat the butter on medium-high speed until it's light and fluffy, about 5 minutes. Stop to scrape down the sides of the bowl to ensure all the butter gets creamed.

8. On medium speed, beat in the cream cheese and vanilla until just combined, about 3 minutes more.

9. Turn the mixer to low speed and add the powdered sugar, about 1 cup at a time, and mix until incorporated.

10. Use an offset spatula or spoon to spread swoopy swirls of frosting all over the cake.

11. Stir the jam with a spoon to loosen it up. Warm it in the microwave for 10 to 20 seconds to help thin it out if needed. Drizzle spoonfuls of jam in lines across the frosting. Draw the tip of an offset spatula (or just use the spoon) to swirl the jam through the frosting. (As seen in the Blackberry-Cashew Sheet Cake picture in the photo insert.) Cut into 18 large or 24 smaller pieces.

12. Store the cake, covered, at room temperature for up to 8 hours and in the fridge overnight or up to 3 days.

Fear-of-Success Snack Cakes

SCHOOL PARTY CUPCAKES
Makes 24 cupcakes

This may be the one instance where you can relate to me on the whole baking-to-avoid-other-baking thing. Is there any other time to bake a cake or cupcakes for a school event other than 9 p.m. the night before? Of course not. And if you don't have the task of baking for school-related activities, then I hope these cupcakes trigger happy memories for you. I was always exceptionally excited when I saw a classmate arrive at school holding a floppy shirt box draped with plastic wrap. I knew we'd be putting down the pencils early and enjoying a sweet treat that afternoon. This whole procrastibaking thing starts young . . .

If you'll be traveling with your cupcakes, avoid disaster and pick up a cupcake carrier or large storage container at your local big-box store.

CUPCAKES

3 cups cake flour

1½ teaspoons baking powder

½ teaspoon baking soda

1 teaspoon kosher salt

1 cup rainbow sprinkles, plus more for garnish

1½ cups buttermilk

1½ cups granulated sugar

¾ cup vegetable oil

4 large eggs

1 tablespoon pure vanilla extract

FROSTING

8 tablespoons (4 ounces) unsalted butter, at room temperature

4 ounces vegetable shortening (or more butter)

2 teaspoons pure vanilla extract

⅛ teaspoon kosher salt

3½ cups powdered sugar

2 to 4 tablespoons whole milk

1. Position a rack in the center of the oven and heat the oven to 325°F. Line two standard muffin pans with paper liners.

2. Make the cupcakes: In a large bowl, whisk together the cake flour, baking powder, baking soda, salt, and sprinkles.

3. In a smaller bowl or large glass measuring cup, whisk together the buttermilk, granulated sugar, oil, eggs, and vanilla.

4. Pour the wet ingredients into the dry and fold to combine. Fill the muffin cups three-quarters full.

5. Bake, rotating the pans front to back halfway through, until the cupcakes have domed and spring back to the touch, 15 to 18 minutes.

6. Allow the cupcakes to cool in the pans for a few minutes before turning out onto a rack to finish cooling. Cool completely before frosting.

7. Make the frosting: In a stand mixer fitted with the paddle (or in a large bowl if using an electric hand mixer), beat the butter on medium-high speed until smooth and no small lumps remain, 2 to 3 minutes. Stop and scrape down the sides of the bowl and add the vegetable shortening, vanilla, and salt. Beat until the mixture is fluffy and lighter in color, stopping to scrape down the sides of the bowl, 3 to 5 minutes.

8. Turn the mixer to low speed and slowly add the powdered sugar until just combined. Stop and scrape down the sides of the bowl, then turn the mixer up to medium and beat until the frosting is bright white and fluffy, 3 to 5 minutes.

9. With the mixer on low speed, add the milk, 1 tablespoon at a time, until your desired frosting consistency is achieved.

10. Spread or pipe the buttercream onto the cupcakes. Garnish with more sprinkles. Cupcakes are best enjoyed the day they're baked, but can be stored in an airtight container at room temperature for up to 2 days.

Fear-of-Success Snack Cakes

CHOCOLATE STOUT CUPCAKES
Makes 24 cupcakes

Even though there's a full cup of beer in these cupcakes, you wouldn't know it at first bite. The dark stout helps to deepen the flavor of the chocolate and adds a tenderness to the cake's crumb. If you don't do alcohol, swap in chilled black coffee.

CHOCOLATE STOUT CUPCAKES

1½ sticks (6 ounces) unsalted butter, at room temperature

1 cup stout beer (like Guinness)

1 cup dark brown sugar

1 cup granulated sugar

1 cup Dutch-process cocoa powder

2 large eggs

½ cup sour cream

2 teaspoons pure vanilla extract

2 cups all-purpose flour

1½ teaspoons baking soda

1 teaspoon baking powder

1 teaspoon kosher salt

COOKED MILK FROSTING

2½ cups whole milk

2½ cups granulated sugar

6 tablespoons cornstarch

¼ teaspoon kosher salt

1 tablespoon pure vanilla extract

5 sticks (20 ounces) unsalted butter, at room temperature

Sprinkles or shaved chocolate, for garnish (optional)

1. Position a rack in the center of the oven and heat the oven to 350°F. Line two standard muffin pans with paper liners.

2. Make the cupcakes: In a small saucepan (or a heatproof bowl if using the microwave), melt the butter and beer together over medium heat. Pour the mixture into a large bowl. Add the brown sugar, granulated sugar, and cocoa powder. Whisk to combine.

3. Add the eggs, one at a time, whisking after each addition. Whisk in the sour cream and vanilla to combine.

4. In a separate large bowl, whisk together the flour, baking soda, baking powder, and salt.

5. Pour the wet ingredients into the dry and stir to combine. Fill the muffin cups three-quarters full.

6. Bake, rotating the pans front to back halfway through, until the cupcakes have domed and spring back to the touch, 12 to 15 minutes.

7. Allow the cupcakes to cool in the pans for a few minutes before turning out onto a rack to finish cooling. Cool completely before frosting.

8. Make the cooked milk frosting: In a medium microwave-safe bowl, whisk together the milk, granulated sugar, cornstarch, and salt. Heat the mixture in the microwave for 2 minutes. Stir well with a rubber spatula. Repeat this process two to three times, until the mixture has thickened to the consistency of mayonnaise. (Alternatively, cook in a medium saucepan over medium-high heat while constantly stirring.) Whisk in the vanilla.

9. In a stand mixer fitted with the paddle (or in a large bowl if using an electric hand mixer), beat the butter on medium-high speed, stopping to scrape down the sides of the bowl, until light and fluffy, 3 to 5 minutes.

10. Turn the mixer to low and add the cooked milk mixture to the creamed butter, a little at a time, until fully incorporated. Turn the mixer to medium-high and beat until light and fluffy, 3 to 5 minutes.

11. Spread or pipe the buttercream onto the cupcakes. Leave them plain or garnish with sprinkles or shaved chocolate.

12. Store in an airtight container at room temperature for up to 8 hours, and in the fridge for up to 3 days.

Fear-of-Success Snack Cakes

TROPICAL CARROT CAKE
Makes 18 to 24 servings

This isn't your typical carrot cake. Getting that out of the way right from the jump, so you don't go into this recipe expecting a classic, layered cake with cream cheese frosting and tiny buttercream carrots piped around the edge. This carrot cake is snazzier, sassier. It's a modern carrot cake living its life in a modern baking world. The batter takes a little longer than typical to put together, but the bright, nutty, familiar-but-updated flavor at the end makes it all worthwhile.

CAKE

2¼ cups all-purpose flour

1 cup unsweetened flake coconut, toasted

1 cup macadamia nuts, toasted

¾ cup crystallized ginger

1 tablespoon ground cinnamon

2½ teaspoons baking powder

½ teaspoon baking soda

1 teaspoon kosher salt

2 cups granulated sugar

1 cup coconut oil, melted

4 large eggs

1 cup sour cream

2 teaspoons pure vanilla extract

2 cups finely grated carrots

1 cup canned crushed pineapple, drained

YOGURT ICING

¼ cup whole-milk Greek yogurt

1 teaspoon pure vanilla extract

2½ cups powdered sugar

Toasted macadamia nuts and toasted flake coconut, for garnish

1. Position a rack in the center of the oven and heat the oven to 350°F. Grease and flour a 13 x 9-inch baking dish.

2. Make the cake: In a food processor, pulse the flour, coconut, macadamia nuts, and ginger until sandy with tiny bits of ginger no larger than a pea. Stop and scrape down the sides of the bowl with a rubber spatula as needed. Pour the mixture into a large bowl.

3. Add the cinnamon, baking powder, baking soda, and salt and whisk to combine.

4. In a small bowl or large glass measuring cup, whisk together the granulated sugar and oil. Whisk in the eggs, sour cream, and vanilla until combined.

5. Pour the wet ingredients into the dry and fold together with a rubber spatula. When a few flour streaks remain, add the carrots and pineapple and fold to combine. Pour the batter into the prepared pan and spread it level.

6. Bake, rotating the pan front to back halfway through, until a toothpick inserted in the center comes out clean or with a few crumbs clinging to it, 35 to 40 minutes.

7. Transfer the pan to a rack to cool until the pan is cool enough to handle. Carefully turn the cake out and return it to the rack. Allow the cake to cool completely before icing.

8. Make the yogurt icing: In a small bowl, whisk together the yogurt, vanilla, and powdered sugar until smooth. Spread the icing over the cake. Garnish with macadamia nuts and coconut.

9. Store, covered, at room temperature for up to 8 hours, and in the fridge overnight or up to 3 days.

There are so many plant-based ingredients in this recipe, it's practically a salad.

CHOCOLATE-CHERRY HI-HAT CUPCAKES
Makes 24 cupcakes

Hi-hat cupcakes are definitely more time-consuming and lots more fun to make than standard cupcakes. The Swiss meringue buttercream isn't as sweet as standard American buttercream, so it plays well with the addition of sweet jam and a crisp chocolate coating. Switch up the flavor of the jam to re-create the flavors of your favorite chocolate-dipped fruit.

CHOCOLATE CUPCAKES

1½ cups all-purpose flour

1 cup granulated sugar

¾ cup Dutch-process cocoa powder

1½ teaspoons baking soda

1 teaspoon baking powder

1 teaspoon kosher salt

¾ cup water

1 teaspoon white vinegar

1 teaspoon pure vanilla extract

3 tablespoons vegetable oil

2 large eggs

CHERRY BUTTERCREAM

½ cup pasteurized egg whites, or 4 large egg whites

1 cup granulated sugar

¼ teaspoon kosher salt

4 sticks (16 ounces) unsalted butter, cold and cubed

1 tablespoon pure vanilla extract

1 cup cherry preserves

COATING

10 ounces semisweet chocolate

2 tablespoons coconut oil or shortening

1. Position two racks in the top and bottom thirds of the oven and heat the oven to 350°F. Line two standard muffin pans with paper liners.

2. Make the cupcakes: In a large bowl, combine the flour, sugar, cocoa powder, baking soda, baking powder, and salt and whisk to combine.

3. In a smaller bowl or large glass measuring cup, whisk together the water, vinegar, vanilla, vegetable oil, and eggs.

4. Pour the wet ingredients over the dry and whisk until just combined. Fill the muffin cups three-quarters full.

5. Bake, rotating the pans front to back halfway through, until the cupcakes have domed and spring back to the touch, 12 to 15 minutes.

6. Allow the cupcakes to cool in the pans for a few minutes before turning out onto a rack to finish cooling. Cool completely before frosting.

7. Make the cherry buttercream: In a medium microwave-safe bowl, whisk together the egg whites, sugar, and salt. Heat the mixture in the microwave on high for 1 minute at a time, whisking after each interval, until the sugar has dissolved, 2 to 3 minutes. (Alternatively, heat the mixture in a heatproof bowl set over a pan of simmering water, whisking occasionally, until the sugar has dissolved.) If you're using fresh egg whites, heat the mixture until it registers 160°F on a candy thermometer.

8. Pour the egg mixture into a stand mixer fitted with the whisk (or in a large bowl if using an electric hand mixer). Whip the egg whites on low speed just until the mixture starts to loosen and foam. Turn the mixer to high speed and beat the egg whites until they resemble a white, fluffy cloud, 8 to 10 minutes.

9. Turn the mixer to low speed and add the butter, a few cubes at a time. The mixture will appear curdled, but that's okay. Once all the butter has been added, turn the mixer up to medium-high speed and whip until the buttercream is smooth, glossy, and light in color, 8 to 10 minutes. Add the vanilla and cherry preserves and mix to combine.

10. Transfer the buttercream to a large piping bag and snip the tip to create a nickel-size opening. Pipe tall swirls on each of the cupcakes and chill until the buttercream is firm, about 30 minutes.

11. Make the coating: Melt the chocolate and coconut oil in a heatproof bowl set over a pan of simmering water (or in the microwave on high in 25-second increments, stirring after each, about 1 minute total). Pull a few cupcakes from the fridge just before you're going to dip them and work in batches. Flip a cupcake upside down and dip the buttercream into the melted chocolate. Shake off the excess and set on a baking sheet or platter. Repeat with the rest of the cupcakes.

12. Store in an airtight container at room temperature for up to 8 hours, or in the fridge for up to 3 days.

Fear-of-Success Snack Cakes

CHEESECAKE-STUFFED NUTELLA COFFEE CAKE
Makes 10 servings

This recipe was a rabbit hole unto itself. I just kept asking myself, "What more could I do to already awesome coffee cake?" Add Nutella? Yep. Stuff it with cheesecake? Check. Top it off with a crunchy, buttery crumble? You betcha. This is the coffee cake dreams are made of. It's a decadent breakfast any day of the week, but also makes for the most amazing afternoon snack. There is no bad time for Cheesecake-Stuffed Nutella Coffee Cake.

Who invented Nutella and where do I send the thank-you note?

CHEESECAKE FILLING

8 ounces cream cheese, at room temperature

½ cup granulated sugar

1 large egg

1 teaspoon pure vanilla extract

CRUMBLE TOPPING

4 tablespoons (2 ounces) unsalted butter, at room temperature

¼ cup granulated sugar

¼ cup dark brown sugar

½ cup all-purpose flour

¼ teaspoon kosher salt

¼ cup chopped hazelnuts

½ teaspoon pure vanilla extract

CAKE

1½ sticks (6 ounces) unsalted butter, at room temperature

6 ounces Nutella or other chocolate-hazelnut spread

⅓ cup granulated sugar

1 teaspoon pure vanilla extract

1½ teaspoons baking powder

1 teaspoon kosher salt

5 large eggs

¾ cup cake flour

1. Make the cheesecake filling: In a stand mixer fitted with the paddle (or in a medium bowl if using an electric hand mixer), beat together the cream cheese and granulated sugar, stopping to scrape down the sides of the bowl to make sure there are no cream cheese lumps.

2. Add the egg and vanilla until completely combined, stopping to scrape down the sides of the bowl one last time. Set the cheesecake batter aside.

3. Make the crumble topping: In a medium bowl, combine the butter, granulated sugar, brown sugar, flour, salt, hazelnuts, and vanilla. Use your immaculately clean fingertips to pinch and toss all of the ingredients together until just combined. The mixture should have a loose, sandy consistency. Set the crumble aside.

4. Position a rack in the center of the oven and heat the oven to 350°F. Line the bottom of a 9-inch round cake pan with a round of parchment paper. Grease the bottom of the pan before adding the paper to help it stick. Grease and flour the paper and sides of the pan.

5. Make the cake: In a stand mixer fitted with the paddle (or in a large bowl if using an electric hand mixer), beat together the butter, Nutella, granulated sugar, vanilla, baking powder, and salt at medium speed until well incorporated and lighter in color, stopping to scrape down the sides of the bowl with a rubber spatula to make sure there are no butter lumps, 3 to 5 minutes.

6. Add the eggs, one at a time, until completely combined. Stop and scrape down the sides of the bowl halfway through mixing and after adding the last egg.

7. With the mixer on low, slowly add the cake flour to the butter mixture until just incorporated. Scrape down the sides of the bowl one last time. Fold in any remaining streaks of flour by hand.

8. Pour half of the batter into the prepared pan. Carefully spoon the cheesecake filling into the pan to cover the layer of Nutella cake batter. Spoon the rest of the Nutella batter over the cheesecake filling and carefully spread to cover. Sprinkle the crumble over the batter.

9. Bake, rotating the pan front to back halfway through, until a toothpick inserted in the center of the cake comes out clean or with a few crumbs clinging to it, 40 to 45 minutes.

10. Transfer the cake to a rack to cool until the pan is cool enough to handle. To turn the cake out, grab two plates. Place one of the plates on top of the cake. Flip the cake over and remove the baking pan. Place the other plate upside down onto the bottom of the cake and flip the whole thing over. Serve immediately or store, covered, at room temperature for up to 8 hours, or in the fridge overnight or up to 3 days.

Fear-of-Success Snack Cakes

CHAPTER 7:

Thanks-for-Your-Patience Pies and Tarts

IF YOU WERE A PIECE OF PIE,
WHAT KIND OF PIE WOULD YOU BE?

IF YOU'RE SMART, YOU'LL BAKE A TART, AVOIDING PROJECTS LEFT TO START. Perhaps a pie to pass the time? A pie right now sure sounds sublime. If baking isn't on the list, then maybe do some more of this. Try and write your work in prose! Send some emails, see how it goes. I'm confident in no time flat your boss, mom, and the cat will suggest you take some time to rest. After all, they know best. And while you rest, here's what you'll do: you'll bake a pie or tart or two.

SPIKED NO-BAKE COOKIES-N-CREAM PIE

Serves 6 to 8

Sometimes you want pie and sometimes you want cheesecake and sometimes you don't want to turn the oven on. This pie is here for you all of those times. Double Stuf Oreos are my favorite cookies to use here and Kahlúa, my favorite liqueur for the job , but you can mix it up with some of the wild new cookie flavors they've been coming out with lately and your booze of choice. If you truly can't be bothered, I also won't be bothered if you use a store-bought crust. The alcohol in this spiked pie never gets cooked out (#blessed). Omit if your crowd is under twenty-one. This recipe produces a gloriously mounded pie; halve the no-bake cheesecake recipe if you want your filling level with the crust.

Who was the evil genius who invented frozen whipped topping?

CRUST

1½ cups chocolate wafer crumbs

⅓ cup granulated sugar

6 tablespoons (3 ounces) unsalted butter, melted

NO-BAKE CHEESECAKE FILLING

16 ounces cream cheese, at room temperature

12 Double Stuf Oreos

2 tablespoons Kahlúa (or your favorite liqueur)

1 teaspoon pure vanilla extract

½ teaspoon kosher salt

1½ cups powdered sugar

3 cups thawed whipped topping or freshly whipped cream

FOR SERVING

Whipped topping or whipped cream

Double Stuf Oreos

1. Make the crust: In a large bowl, stir together the chocolate wafer crumbs, granulated sugar, and melted butter.

2. Press the mixture into a 9-inch pie pan. Use a glass (or another pie pan) to press the crumbs flat into the bottom and up the sides of the pan. Chill the crust while making the filling.

3. Make the no-bake cheesecake filling: In a stand mixer fitted with the paddle (or in a large bowl if using an electric hand mixer), beat the cream cheese on medium-high speed, stopping to scrape down the sides of the bowl with a rubber spatula, until smooth, 3 to 5 minutes. Add the cookies, liqueur, vanilla, and salt. Mix on low to smash the cookies into chunks.

4. With the mixer on low, slowly add the powdered sugar and mix until combined. Stop and scrape down the sides of the bowl. Fold in the whipped topping by hand.

5. Pour the cheesecake into the crust and smooth the top with an offset spatula. Cover with plastic wrap and freeze for 2 hours, or up to overnight. Allow the pie to thaw in the fridge shortly before serving.

6. Slice with a warm knife, wiping down the blade between cuts. Serve with a dollop of whipped topping and an extra cookie on the side. Store, wrapped, in the fridge for up to 3 days or in the freezer for up to 3 months.

CHOCOLATE-CARAMEL PRETZEL MINI TARTS
Makes 64 mini tarts

You know those no-bake, candy pretzel bites that people make around the holidays? These tarts are their older, cooler cousins from out of town. Plus, they're more time-consuming to make, so you can avoid wrapping presents just a little longer.

2 sticks (8 ounces) unsalted butter, at room temperature

1 cup powdered sugar

1½ teaspoons pure vanilla extract

1 teaspoon kosher salt

2 large egg yolks

2½ cups all-purpose flour

½ cup Dutch-process cocoa powder

64 caramel-filled chocolate candies (like Rolos)

64 mini pretzels

1. Position a rack in the center of the oven and heat the oven to 350°F. Grease the cups of two mini muffin pans.

2. In a stand mixer fitted with the paddle (or in a large bowl if using an electric hand mixer), beat the butter, powdered sugar, vanilla, and salt on medium-high speed, stopping to scrape down the sides of the bowl to make sure there are no butter lumps, until fluffy and lighter in color, 3 to 5 minutes.

3. Add the egg yolks and mix to combine, stopping to scrape down the sides of the bowl.

4. With the mixer on low, slowly add the flour and cocoa powder. Mix just until the dough comes together. Scrape down the bowl one last time and fold in any flour or cocoa streaks by hand.

5. Fill each of the cups of the prepared pan with about ½ tablespoon of dough rolled into a ball. Press the balls flat into the pan.

6. Bake, rotating the pan front to back halfway through, until the cookies have puffed up and lost their raw sheen, 6 to 8 minutes.

7. Transfer the pan to a rack. Bake the second pan while you add the candy to the first pan of tarts. While the tarts are still warm, press a chocolate candy upside down into the center of each tart. Add a pretzel to each tart, making sure it lands in the melted chocolate so it sticks.

8. Allow the tarts to cool in the pan at room temperature until the chocolate from the candies has started to firm back up, about 20 minutes. Carefully remove them from the pan using a small offset spatula or butter knife. Repeat the baking and cooling process with the remaining dough.

9. Store in an airtight container at room temperature for up to 3 days.

PEACHES AND CREAM PAVLOVA
Serves 6 to 8

If you've never made pavlova before, your friends and family are going to think you're a culinary genius after you present this fluffy cloud of creamy, fruity goodness. Classic pavlova employs bananas and passion fruit, but you'll find everyone makes it a little differently. It's one of those recipes that can be reimagined in endless ways and tweaked to use up whatever you have on hand.

MERINGUE

4 large egg whites

Pinch of kosher salt

1 cup granulated sugar

1 teaspoon cornstarch

2 teaspoons white vinegar or lemon juice

1 teaspoon pure vanilla extract

FRUIT

½ cup granulated sugar

2 peaches, sliced

1 teaspoon pure vanilla extract

WHIPPED CREAM

1 cup heavy cream

½ cup powdered sugar

½ teaspoon pure vanilla extract

1. Position a rack in the center of the oven and heat the oven to 250°F. Line a rimmed baking sheet with parchment paper or a silicone baking mat.

2. Make the meringue: In a stand mixer fitted with the whisk (or in a large metal bowl if using an electric hand mixer), whip the egg whites and salt on medium-high speed until soft, glossy peaks form. Slowly pour in the granulated sugar and continue to whip until the whites hold stiff peaks. Sprinkle the cornstarch over the whites and mix on low to combine. Remove the bowl from the mixer and gently fold in the vinegar and vanilla with a rubber spatula.

3. Pour the fluffy meringue onto the prepared baking sheet, mounding it up into a large round 8 to 9 inches in diameter. Use a dinner plate or mixing bowl as your guide.

4. Bake, until the meringue is firm to the touch, 1 hour to 1 hour 30 minutes. Turn the oven off, prop the door open, and allow the meringue to cool in the oven for at least another hour.

5. Meanwhile, prepare the fruit: In a small bowl, combine the granulated sugar, peaches, and vanilla and toss to combine. Set aside.

6. Make the whipped cream: In a stand mixer fitted with the whisk (or in a small bowl if using an electric stand mixer), whip the heavy cream, powdered sugar, and vanilla to soft peaks.

7. Carefully slide the giant meringue onto a serving platter. Don't worry if it cracks a little—this is supposed to be a messier dessert. Right before serving, top with the whipped cream and peaches. Slice the meringue with a chef's knife and scoop servings onto plates using a large serving spoon. Pavlova is best enjoyed shortly after baking.

STONE FRUIT CROSTATA

Serves 6 to 8

A crostata is a rustic, free-form tart, perfect for the days that you feel like baking a pie or tart but don't feel like being perfect. No trimming or weaving with this dough, just scraggly edges that bake up golden and crisp. Use whatever fruit you have on hand. Berries, peaches, apples, or figs all work beautifully.

FILLING

3 cups sliced stone fruit (any combination of plums, peaches, cherries, or nectarines)

½ cup granulated sugar

2 tablespoons cornstarch

1 teaspoon ground cinnamon

1 teaspoon pure vanilla extract

CRUST

2 cups all-purpose flour

½ teaspoon kosher salt

2 tablespoons granulated sugar

8 tablespoons (4 ounces) unsalted butter, cold and cubed

1 large egg yolk

½ cup sour cream

2 tablespoons heavy cream

2 tablespoons turbinado sugar, for sprinkling

Vanilla ice cream, for serving

1. Prepare the filling: In a large bowl, toss the fruit and sugar together. Add the cornstarch, cinnamon, and vanilla and toss to combine.

2. Position a rack in the center of the oven and heat the oven to 350°F. Line a rimmed baking sheet with parchment paper or a silicone baking mat.

3. Make the crust: In a large bowl, whisk together the flour, salt, and granulated sugar. Add the butter. Pinch and press the butter into the flour mixture until it resembles coarse sand.

4. Make a well in the center and add the egg yolk and sour cream. Mix with your hands until a soft dough forms. Turn the dough out onto a floured work surface and roll into a 9-inch round ¼ inch thick.

5. Slide the dough onto the prepared baking sheet. Pile the filling onto the middle of the dough. Fold the edges of the dough up around the filling, overlapping as you go. Brush the sides of the dough with the heavy cream and sprinkle with the turbinado sugar.

6. Bake, rotating the pan front to back halfway through, until the crust is golden brown and the filling is soft and bubbling, 25 to 35 minutes.

7. Serve immediately with a scoop of vanilla ice cream on the side. Store leftover crostata in an airtight container in the fridge for up to 3 days. Rewarm slices in a toaster oven.

CHOCOLATE PUDDING PIE
Serves 6 to 8

It's beloved for a reason: it's really freaking good! I've watched even the most discerning foodies happily scarf down a slice of this American classic. This pie is my husband's favorite, so I make it every Thanksgiving. You don't have to wait for a holiday to whip this up, though. It's just as good on a random Tuesday night. It'll also be our little secret if you decide to pick up a premade crust and boxed pudding mix.

CRUST

1½ cups graham cracker crumbs

⅓ cup granulated sugar

6 tablespoons (3 ounces) unsalted butter, melted

FILLING

3 cups whole milk

1½ teaspoons pure vanilla extract

3 tablespoons cornstarch

4 large egg yolks

¾ cup granulated sugar

¼ teaspoon kosher salt

6 ounces bittersweet chocolate, finely chopped (1¼ cups)

Whipped cream, berries, chocolate shavings, and/or caramel sauce, for serving

1. Position a rack in the center of the oven and heat the oven to 350°F.

2. Make the crust: In a large bowl, stir together the graham cracker crumbs, sugar, and melted butter.

3. Press the mixture into a 9-inch pie pan. Use a glass (or another pie pan) to press the crumbs flat into the bottom and up the sides of the pan.

4. Bake until the crust is set, 7 to 9 minutes. Place the crust on a rack to cool while you make the filling.

5. Make the filling: In a small bowl or measuring cup, whisk together 1 cup of the milk, the vanilla, and cornstarch until smooth. Whisk in the egg yolks, sugar, and salt until combined.

6. Pour the remaining 2 cups milk into a large saucepan and bring to a gentle boil over medium to medium-high heat.

7. When tiny bubbles start to form around the edges of the warming milk, pour in the yolk mixture and whisk until combined. Reduce the heat to medium-low and switch to a silicone spatula. Stir constantly, making sure the spatula scrapes the bottom of the pan, until the custard is the consistency of mayonnaise, 8 to 10 minutes. Remove from the heat and stir in the chocolate until completely combined.

8. Pour the mixture through a fine-mesh sieve directly into the piecrust and smooth the top with an offset spatula. Chill for at least 2 hours, or up to overnight, before serving.

9. Serve with fresh whipped cream, berries, chocolate shavings, or caramel sauce. Store leftovers covered in the fridge for up to 3 days.

If you start to make a tart and realize you don't have the parts, hop online and grab a pan, toss it in that cart and then, have a seat and take a break, it'll be two days till you can bake. While you wait, this maze looks great! Tootle through the heart and back to find yourself a tasty snack.

GAME TIME!

START

BOURBON PECAN TART
Serves 8 to 10

It can be Thanksgiving any day of the year when you make this bourbon pecan tart! I love serving this rich, caramel-y tart with vanilla ice cream or whipped cream. As it bakes, your house will smell like heaven and inspire you to move quickly through whatever it is you've dreaded getting done.

CRUST

1½ sticks (6 ounces) unsalted butter, at room temperature

¼ cup granulated sugar

1 teaspoon pure vanilla extract

½ teaspoon kosher salt

2 cups all-purpose flour

FILLING

1 cup dark brown sugar

1 cup light corn syrup

4 tablespoons (2 ounces) unsalted butter, melted

3 tablespoons bourbon

1 tablespoon grated orange zest

1 teaspoon pure vanilla extract

¼ teaspoon kosher salt

3 large eggs

3 cups pecan halves

1. Make the crust: In a stand mixer fitted with the paddle (or in a large bowl if using an electric hand mixer), beat the butter, granulated sugar, vanilla, and salt on medium-high speed, stopping to scrape down the sides of the bowl, until fluffy and lighter in color, 3 to 5 minutes.

2. With the mixer on low, slowly add the flour until just combined. Scrape down the sides of the bowl one last time and fold in any remaining flour streaks by hand.

3. Turn the dough out onto your work surface and gather it into a smooth disk. Wrap with plastic wrap and chill for at least 1 hour, or up to overnight.

4. Dust your work surface with flour and roll the chilled dough into a 10-inch round. Dust the dough with flour as needed. Roll the dough up onto your rolling pin and unroll it into a 9-inch removable bottom tart pan. Press the dough into the pan and clean up the edges with a sharp knife. Patch up any holes or cracks with extra dough. Freeze the tart shell for 30 minutes before baking.

5. Position a rack in the center of the oven and heat the oven to 350°F.

6. Prick the bottom of the tart shell with the tines of a fork. Press parchment paper into the bottom of the unbaked tart shell and fill with pie weights (dried beans, uncooked rice, etc.).

7. Bake, rotating the pan halfway through, until the crust has just set, 12 to 15 minutes. Remove from the oven but leave the oven on.

8. Transfer the pan to a rack to cool. Remove the pie weights and allow the tart shell to cool while you make the filling.

9. Make the filling: In a large bowl, whisk together the brown sugar, corn syrup, melted butter, bourbon, orange zest, vanilla, and salt. Add the eggs and whisk to combine. Stir in the pecans.

10. Set the tart crust on a baking sheet. Scoop the filling into the crust, nuts first, making sure the pecans are spread out evenly. Pour any liquid left in the bowl over the pecans just until the filling reaches the top of the crust.

11. Bake, rotating the pan front to back halfway through, until the filling is set with the slightest jiggle in the middle, 25 to 30 minutes.

12. Transfer the tart to a rack until cool enough to handle. Carefully remove the tart from the outer ring of the tart pan. Loosen the bottom with a small knife or an offset spatula and slide the tart onto a platter. Serve the tart while still warm. You can also make this tart up to a day in advance and rewarm in a low oven, covered with foil. Wrap leftovers and store in the fridge for up to 3 days. Rewarm leftovers in the toaster oven.

LEMON TART
Serves 8 to 10

This tart is 100 percent made from scratch, but harnesses the power of the microwave in a way that would make any convenience food proud. It might feel wrong to quickly slap together the lemon curd filling in the microwave after lovingly making, chilling, rolling, chilling again, and baking the tart crust, but trust me. It's right. Your arms will be grateful for the break.

CRUST

1½ sticks (6 ounces) unsalted butter, at room temperature

¼ cup granulated sugar

1 teaspoon pure vanilla extract

½ teaspoon kosher salt

2 cups all-purpose flour

LEMON CURD

¾ cup lemon juice

1 large egg

3 large egg yolks

⅔ cup granulated sugar

4 tablespoons (2 ounces) unsalted butter, cubed

Pinch of kosher salt

½ teaspoon pure vanilla extract

Whipped cream, berries, or vanilla ice cream, for serving

1. Make the crust: In a stand mixer fitted with the paddle (or in a large bowl if using an electric hand mixer), beat the butter, sugar, vanilla, and salt on medium-high speed, stopping to scrape down the sides of the bowl, until fluffy and lighter in color, 3 to 5 minutes.

2. With the mixer on low, slowly add the flour until just combined. Scrape down the sides of the bowl one last time and fold in any remaining flour streaks by hand.

3. Turn the dough out onto your work surface and gather it into a smooth disk. Wrap with plastic wrap and chill for at least 1 hour, or up to overnight.

4. Dust your work surface with flour and roll the chilled dough into a 10-inch round. Dust the dough with flour as needed. Roll the disk up onto your rolling pin and unroll it into a 9-inch removable bottom tart pan. Press the dough into the pan and clean up the edges with a sharp knife. Patch up any holes or cracks with extra dough. Freeze the tart shell for 30 minutes before baking.

5. Position a rack in the center of the oven and heat the oven to 350°F.

6. Prick the bottom of the tart shell with the tines of a fork. Press parchment paper into the bottom of the unbaked tart shell and fill with pie weights (dried beans, uncooked rice, etc.).

7. Bake, rotating the pan front to back halfway through, until the crust has started to slightly brown along the edges, 15 to 20 minutes.

8. Leave the oven on and transfer the pan to a rack. Remove the pie weights and return the tart shell to the oven to ensure the center has baked through, 5 to 7 minutes more.

9. Transfer the pan to a rack to cool. Once the pan is cool to the touch, you can move the shell to the fridge to speed up the process.

10. Make the lemon curd: In a large microwave-safe bowl, whisk together the lemon juice, egg, egg yolks, sugar, butter, and salt.

11. Microwave on high for 1 minute. Whisk to distribute the heat. Repeat the heating and whisking process four to five more times, until the mixture has thickened to the consistency of Greek yogurt. Whisk in the vanilla. The curd will continue to thicken as it cools.

12. Pour the lemon curd into the tart shell. Chill in the tart pan for at least 3 hours before serving.

13. Carefully remove the tart from the outer ring of the tart pan. Loosen the bottom with a small knife or an offset spatula and slide the tart onto a platter. Serve with fresh whipped cream, berries, or a scoop of vanilla ice cream. Store leftovers, wrapped, in the fridge for up to 2 days. The crust will soften the longer it sits in the fridge.

 Top your tart with Meringue Kisses (page 83).

Thanks-for-Your-Patience Pies and Tarts

BILLIONAIRE TART
Serves 12 to 15

You may have heard of millionaire bars, consisting of a shortbread crust, caramel filing, and chocolate ganache topping. They're good and all, but these days it's all about the billionaire. Shortbread crust is exchanged for a brownie bottom, topped with creamy caramel, decadent cookie dough, and a layer of milk chocolate to keep it all together. Make these to achieve billionaire status without having to develop your own line of lip kits or engage in any insider trading.

BROWNIE BOTTOM

½ cup vegetable oil

¾ cup Dutch-process cocoa powder

1¼ cups granulated sugar

2 large eggs

½ teaspoon kosher salt

½ teaspoon pure vanilla extract

¾ cup all-purpose flour

CARAMEL FILLING

20 to 30 chewy caramel candies (about 1 cup)

COOKIE DOUGH LAYER

8 tablespoons (4 ounces) unsalted butter, at room temperature

¼ cup granulated sugar

¼ cup dark brown sugar

1 teaspoon pure vanilla extract

2 tablespoons heavy cream

1 teaspoon salt

1 cup all-purpose flour

½ cup semisweet chocolate chips

TOPPING

8 ounces milk chocolate, chopped

2 tablespoons coconut oil

1. Position a rack in the center of the oven and heat the oven to 325°F. Line a 9-inch round cake pan with enough foil to cover the bottom and sides. Grease the foil.

2. Make the brownie bottom: In a small bowl or glass measuring cup, whisk together the vegetable oil, cocoa powder, granulated sugar, eggs, salt, and vanilla. Add the flour and stir to combine.

3. Pour the batter into the prepared pan and bake until the brownie is set, 15 to 20 minutes.

4. Arrange the caramel candies on top of the brownie as soon as it comes out of the oven. Place the pan back into the oven to melt the caramels, 2 to 3 minutes. Spread the melted caramel out with an offset spatula or the back of a spoon.

5. Transfer the pan to a rack until it's cool enough to handle. Then move the pan to the fridge to firm up the caramel.

6. Make the cookie dough layer: In a stand mixer fitted with the paddle (or in a large bowl if using an electric hand mixer), beat the butter, granulated sugar, brown sugar, vanilla, heavy cream, and salt on medium-high speed, stopping to scrape down the sides of the bowl to make sure there are no butter lumps, until light and fluffy, 3 to 5 minutes.

7. With the mixer on low, slowly add the flour and chocolate chips and mix to combine.

8. Spoon the dough onto the caramel layer and spread it out using an offset spatula or back of a spoon.

9. Make the topping: Melt the chocolate and coconut oil in a heatproof bowl set over a pan of simmering water (or in the microwave on high in 25-second increments, stirring after each, about 1 minute total). Spread the melted chocolate out over the top of the cookie dough. Return the pan to the fridge for at least 30 minutes, or up to overnight, before serving.

10. Use the foil to lift the tart from the pan. Slice thin wedges with a warm knife. Store, covered with plastic wrap, at room temperature for up to 3 days, or in the fridge for a week.

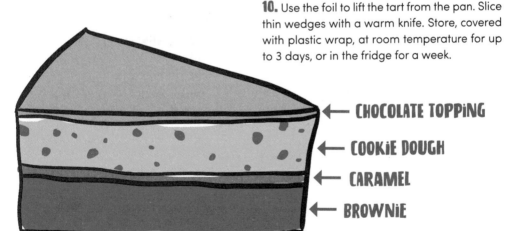

← CHOCOLATE TOPPING

← COOKIE DOUGH

← CARAMEL

← BROWNIE

Thanks-for-Your-Patience Pies and Tarts

BOSTON CREAM TART
Serves 8 to 10

Add some pastry cream, ganache, and toasted almonds and literally anything can become the Boston Cream variation of itself. The tart variation of this makeover is perfect to serve as part of a brunch spread or holiday dessert table. The combination of simple, satisfying flavors is sure to please most.

 Why do they call it Boston Cream Pie when it's really a cake?

CRUST

1½ sticks (6 ounces) unsalted butter, at room temperature

¼ cup granulated sugar

1 teaspoon pure vanilla extract

½ teaspoon kosher salt

2 cups all-purpose flour

PASTRY CREAM

6 large egg yolks

⅔ cup granulated sugar

3 tablespoons cornstarch

Pinch of kosher salt

2 cups whole milk

1 tablespoon unsalted butter

1 tablespoon pure vanilla extract

TOPPING

6 ounces bittersweet chocolate, chopped

⅔ cup heavy cream

3 ounces white chocolate, melted (optional)

½ cup sliced almonds, toasted

Whipped cream, fresh berries, or caramel sauce, for serving

1. Make the crust: In a stand mixer fitted with the paddle (or in a large bowl if using an electric hand mixer), beat the butter, sugar, vanilla, and salt on medium-high speed, stopping to scrape down the sides of the bowl, until fluffy and lighter in color, 3 to 5 minutes.

2. With the mixer on low, slowly add the flour until just combined. Scrape down the sides of the bowl one last time and fold in any remaining flour streaks by hand.

3. Turn the dough out onto your work surface and gather it into a smooth disk. Wrap with plastic wrap and chill for at least 1 hour, or up to overnight.

4. Dust your work surface with flour and roll the chilled dough into a 10-inch round. Dust the dough with flour as needed. Roll the dough up onto your rolling pin and unroll it into a 9-inch removable bottom tart pan. Press the dough into the pan and clean up the edges with a sharp knife. Patch up any holes or cracks with extra dough. Freeze the tart shell for 30 minutes before baking.

5. Position a rack in the center of the oven and heat the oven to 350°F.

6. Prick the bottom of the tart shell with the tines of a fork. Press parchment paper into the bottom of the unbaked tart shell and fill with pie weights (dried beans, uncooked rice, etc.).

7. Bake, rotating the pan front to back halfway through, until the crust has started to turn golden brown, 15 to 20 minutes.

8. Leave the oven on and transfer the pan to a rack. Remove the pie weights and return the tart shell to the oven to ensure the center has baked through, 5 to 7 more minutes.

9. Transfer the pan to a rack to cool. Once the pan is cool to the touch, you can move the shell to the fridge to speed up the process.

10. Make the pastry cream: In a large heat-proof bowl, whisk together the egg yolks, sugar, cornstarch, and salt.

11. In a medium saucepan, bring the milk to a boil over medium-high heat. Remove from the heat. Slowly add half of the milk to the egg mixture while whisking vigorously to combine. Pour the tempered egg mixture back into the hot milk.

12. Cook over medium-low heat, stirring constantly with a heatproof silicone spatula, until thickened to the texture of mayonnaise, about 5 minutes.

13. Strain the pastry cream through a fine-mesh sieve into a medium bowl. Add the butter and vanilla and whisk until combined.

14. Fill the tart shell no more than three-quarters full with the pastry cream, leaving space at the top for the ganache. Transfer to the fridge to allow the pastry cream to cool completely before adding the ganache, 10 to 15 minutes.

15. Make the topping: Place the chocolate in a small heatproof bowl. Scald the heavy cream in a coffee mug in the microwave or in a small saucepan over medium-low heat. Pour the heavy cream over the chocolate and whisk until smooth.

16. Carefully spread the ganache over the pastry cream and smooth the top with an offset spatula. If desired, drizzle melted white chocolate in lines over the warm ganache. Quickly draw the tip of a knife back and forth through the lines to create a zigzag pattern. Sprinkle the almonds around the edges of the tart.

17. Chill until the ganache has set firm, at least 30 minutes.

18. Slice with a warm knife and serve with whipped cream, berries, or caramel sauce. Leftovers can be stored in an airtight container in the fridge for up to 3 days. The tart crust will soften the longer it sits in the fridge.

CARAMEL APPLE SLAB PIE
Serves 24 to 30

Slab pies, in my humble opinion, contain the perfect crust-to-filling ratio. That is, lots of crust to a little filling. Since you're baking in such a large pan, this pie will serve a much larger crowd than a standard round. It's ideal if you have lots of people coming and going around the holidays.

CARAMEL SAUCE

¾ cup granulated sugar

¼ cup water

Pinch of cream of tartar

½ teaspoon kosher salt

¼ cup heavy cream

3 tablespoons (1½ ounces) unsalted butter

½ teaspoon pure vanilla extract

PIE DOUGH

7½ cups all-purpose flour

1 tablespoon kosher salt

½ cup granulated sugar

5 sticks (20 ounces) unsalted butter, cold and cubed

¾ cup ice water

FILLING

20 apples, peeled and thinly sliced

3 tablespoons lemon juice

2 cups granulated sugar

3 tablespoons cornstarch

1 teaspoon kosher salt

1 teaspoon ground cinnamon

¼ teaspoon ground allspice

GLAZE

1 large egg yolk

¼ cup heavy cream

¼ cup granulated sugar

1. Make the caramel sauce: In a small saucepan, combine the sugar, water, cream of tartar, and salt. Cook over medium-high heat without stirring until dark amber in color, about 5 minutes.

2. Remove the pan from the heat and carefully whisk in the heavy cream. The caramel will sputter and release steam as the cream is added.

3. Whisk in the butter and vanilla. Set the caramel sauce aside to cool while you make the pie. Caramel sauce can be made up to 3 days in advance and held in the fridge in an airtight container.

4. Make the pie dough: In a large bowl, combine the flour, salt, and sugar and whisk to combine. Add the butter to the flour. Pinch and press the butter pieces into the flour until the mixture resembles coarse sand.

5. Make a well in the center of the flour and add half of the ice water. Gently work the water into the flour, adding more as needed, until a dough forms.

6. Dust your work surface with flour and turn the dough out onto the surface. Gently knead it a few times until smooth. Divide the dough into two unequal disks, about two-thirds and one-third. Wrap with plastic wrap and chill for 30 minutes, or up to overnight.

7. Position a rack in the center of the oven and heat the oven to 375°F. Have a rimmed baking sheet nearby.

8. Dust your work surface with flour and roll out the bigger piece of dough into a ¼-inch-thick rectangle about 20 x 15 inches, or at least 2 inches longer on all sides than the pan you are using. Dust the top of the dough with flour and carefully fold in half, then fold in half again. Use a bench scraper to help you lift the folded dough into the rimmed baking sheet. Unfold the dough and press into the bottom and sides of the pan. Trim away the excess and reserve the dough scraps. Repair any holes or cracks with extra dough. Set the pie shell aside.

9. Make the filling: In a large bowl, combine the apple slices and lemon juice and toss to combine. Add the sugar, cornstarch, salt, cinnamon, and allspice and toss to combine.

10. Pour the filling into the pie shell and spread it out evenly. Drizzle the caramel sauce over the apples.

11. Roll the second disc of dough to about ¼-inch thick and cut into long strips. You can make your lattice however you like, but to make it similar to the picture of the Caramel Apple Slab Pie in the photo insert, cut your strips in varying widths, ½ to 1½ inches wide.

12. Add diagonal strips to the pan, alternating thick and thin pieces, about 2 inches apart so the filling shows through. Place another layer of strips diagonally in the other direction, but weave them one at a time: Start with a central strip angled from corner to corner, weaving it under and over the strips in the lower layer. Continue weaving more strips 2 inches apart, alternating thick and thin pieces. Gather and reroll dough as needed to cut out more strips. Press the strips and bottom layer of dough together all around the edges and trim away the excess.

13. Make the glaze: In a small bowl, whisk together the egg yolk and cream.

14. Optional decoration: Gather and reroll the reserved dough scraps, flouring as needed. Cut 3 dozen small leaves. Stick the leaves around the edges of the pie and randomly on the strips (or to cover tears), using a dab of the egg wash as glue.

15. Brush away any excess flour, then coat thoroughly with the egg wash. Sprinkle with the sugar.

16. Bake for 30 minutes, checking around the 20-minute mark to see how dark the crust has browned. Tent the pie with foil when the crust reaches a deep, golden brown color. Continue baking until the filling is golden and bubbling, 10 to 15 minutes more.

17. Set the pan on a rack to cool. Store leftovers covered with plastic wrap in the fridge for up to 3 days. The crust will soften the longer it sits in the fridge. Rewarm leftovers in the toaster oven.

Thanks-for-Your-Patience Pies and Tarts

CHAPTER 8:

Sorry-for-the-Delayed-Response Savory Bakes

IF YOU WERE A SAVORY TREAT, WHAT KIND OF SAVORY TREAT WOULD YOU BE?

AS SOMEONE WHO SPENDS A GREAT DEAL OF TIME BAKING FOR BOTH BUSINESS AND PLEASURE, IT'S REFRESHING AND NECESSARY FOR ME TO TAKE A WALK ON THE SAVORY SIDE FROM TIME TO TIME. All that sugary sweetness needs to be balanced by a little cheesy, salty goodness. A perk of savory procrastibaking: sides for your next dinner party or lunch on the go.

PIZZA PALMIERS

Makes 24 palmiers

There are themes that run through the baking I do for my own enjoyment, like pizza. I blame my New Jersey upbringing. Palmiers are a whimsical-looking coiled pastry that can be made sweet or savory depending on what you stuff them with. They're fun to say, fun to eat, and offer varying levels of time investment. I typically make these with puff pastry purchased at the store, but you are more than welcome to make your own if you want to jump down that rabbit hole. Swap in your favorite pizza toppings for the pepperoni or change things altogether by filling the palmiers with spinach and artichoke dip or hummus and olives. Serve these little pizza wheels for dinner with a side salad, as a party appetizer, or on game day. If you're uncharacteristically thinking ahead, freeze the wrapped rolls at the end of step 4. Slice straight from the freezer and bake immediately. Frozen rolls will just take a minute or two longer to bake.

8 ounces cream cheese, at room temperature

1 teaspoon dried oregano

1 teaspoon dried thyme

1 teaspoon garlic powder

1 cup marinara sauce

1 cup shredded mozzarella cheese

½ cup grated Parmesan cheese

All-purpose flour, for dusting

2 sheets frozen puff pastry, thawed

6 ounces sliced pepperoni, chopped (optional)

1. In a medium bowl, use a fork to mash together the cream cheese, oregano, thyme, garlic powder, marinara sauce, mozzarella, and half of the Parmesan until combined.

2. Dust your work surface with flour and roll or trim (depending on the size of your dough) one of the pastry sheets into an 11 x 9-inch rectangle.

3. Spread half of the pizza mixture evenly over the dough and sprinkle with half of the chopped pepperoni (if using).

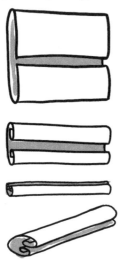

4. Rolling up the dough is easier to do than to explain. With one of the short sides of dough facing you, imagine a horizontal centerline running through the middle of the dough dividing it into an upper and a lower section. Working with the lower section first, fold the end into the center of that section. Then fold that same piece of dough again so that it touches the centerline. (Fold, fold, center.) If you look at it from the side, you should see three layers of dough coiled up. Repeat the same process with the upper section. Then, bring the two rolled portions of dough together, just like closing a book. Slide the roll onto a baking sheet. Repeat the whole process with the other sheet of dough. Store, wrapped, in the fridge for at least 1 hour before baking, or up to overnight.

5. Position two racks in the top and bottom thirds of the oven and heat the oven to 400°F. Line two baking sheets with parchment paper or silicone baking mats.

6. Slice the chilled rolls crosswise into ¾-inch-thick pieces. Place cut side down on the prepared baking sheets and space at least 2 inches apart. Sprinkle with the remaining Parmesan.

7. Bake, rotating the pans front to back halfway through, until the palmiers have puffed up and are golden brown along the edges, 12 to 16 minutes.

8. Palmiers are best enjoyed shortly after baking, but can be stored in an airtight container in the fridge for up to 3 days. Rewarm in the toaster or a warm oven before serving.

Hop on YouTube and watch pastry chefs of all kinds all over the world rolling up their palmiers.

Roll up your sleeves, call in sick, and make your own puff pastry.

CHEDDAR-PEPPER CORN BREAD

Makes 9 servings

ROASTED VEGETABLES

2 tablespoons finely diced shallot (or whatever onion you have on hand)

1 cup diced red bell pepper

Extra-virgin olive oil

Salt and ground black pepper

CORN BREAD

1½ cups all-purpose flour

1 cup cornmeal

¼ cup granulated sugar

2 teaspoons baking powder

¼ teaspoon baking soda

1 teaspoon kosher salt

½ teaspoon ground black pepper

1¼ cups whole milk

½ cup corn oil (or whatever vegetable oil you have on hand)

2 large eggs

1 cup shredded cheddar cheese

1. Position a rack in the center of the oven and heat the oven to 400°F.

2. Roast the vegetables: Toss the shallot and bell pepper onto a baking sheet. Drizzle with enough olive oil to coat and sprinkle with salt and black pepper to taste. Roast until softened, 10 to 15 minutes. Transfer the baking sheet to a rack to cool.

3. Leave the oven on, but reduce the temperature to 375°F. Grease an 8-inch square baking dish.

4. Make the corn bread: In a large bowl, whisk together the flour, cornmeal, sugar, baking powder, baking soda, salt, and black pepper.

5. In a small bowl or large glass measuring cup, whisk together the milk, corn oil, and eggs.

6. Pour the wet ingredients, roasted vegetables, and cheddar into the dry. Fold to combine. Pour the batter into the prepared pan.

7. Bake, rotating the pan front to back halfway through, until a toothpick inserted in the middle comes out clean or with a few crumbs clinging to it, 20 to 25 minutes.

8. Transfer the baking dish to a rack to cool for a few minutes before cutting. Corn bread is best enjoyed shortly after it's made, but can be stored in an airtight container at room temperature for up to 2 days. Enjoy at room temperature or rewarm in the toaster oven. Adding a dab of butter or olive oil before warming will help keep the bread tender.

EVERYTHING SWEET POTATO BISCUITS
Makes 12 large biscuits

The addition of mashed sweet potato and "everything" seasoning helps elevate the simple biscuit to something worthy of building a meal around. These biscuits are perfect for dipping in soups or using as the vessel in a bacon, egg, and cheese sandwich. The savory "everything" seasoning blend balances well with the sweetness the sweet potato lends to the dough. If you don't have all the spices to make the blend, at the very least sprinkle with generous pinches of salt and ground black pepper.

"EVERYTHING" SEASONING BLEND

2 tablespoons coarse salt or pretzel salt

2 tablespoons minced dried garlic

1½ tablespoons dried onion flakes

1½ tablespoons sesame seeds

1 tablespoon poppy seeds

BISCUITS

3 cups all-purpose flour

1 tablespoon baking powder

¾ teaspoon baking soda

1 teaspoon kosher salt

¼ cup dark brown sugar

1½ sticks (6 ounces) unsalted butter, cold and cubed

1 cup mashed sweet potato

½ cup heavy cream, cold, plus more for brushing

1. Make the "everything" seasoning blend: In a small bowl, stir together the salt, garlic, onion flakes, sesame seeds, and poppy seeds. Store in an airtight container in the pantry for up to 6 months.

2. Position a rack in the center of the oven and heat the oven to 375°F. Line a baking sheet with parchment paper or a silicone baking mat.

3. Make the biscuits: In a medium bowl, whisk together the flour, baking powder, baking soda, salt, and brown sugar.

4. Add the cubed butter to the flour mixture. Pinch and press the cold butter cubes into the dry ingredients until the mixture is sandy in texture.

5. Make a well in the middle of the mixture and add the mashed sweet potato and heavy cream. Gently fold the mixture together with your hands until a soft dough forms.

6. Dust your work surface with flour and turn the sweet potato dough out onto the surface. Lightly dust the top of the dough with flour.

7. Before cutting it into biscuits, you're first going to fold the dough like you'd fold a business letter. Do this by pressing the dough into a 12 x 6-inch rectangle (doesn't have to be exact). With a long side facing you, imagine three horizontal lines dividing the length of the dough into thirds (again, think of a business letter). You can even gently score the dough if that helps you visualize it better. Carefully lift up one of the short ends of dough and fold it onto the middle third of dough. Lift up the other short end and fold it over the middle third of dough. You should now have three distinct layers of dough in a smaller rectangle.

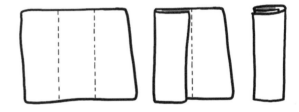

8. Lightly press the dough down until it's about ½ inch thick. Cut the dough into 12 squares and move them to the lined baking sheet. Brush the tops with cream and dust them with the "everything" seasoning blend.

9. Bake, rotating the pan front to back halfway through, until puffed up and the edges have just started to brown, 8 to 10 minutes.

10. Biscuits are best enjoyed shortly after baking, but can be stored in an airtight container for up to 2 days.

Not sure how to mash a sweet potato? Scrub the skin clean, prick all over with the tines of a fork, and nuke it on high for 5 minutes.

30 MINUTES

LEMON-PEPPER CRACKERS
Makes about 24 small crackers

Once you figure out that you can make your own crackers at home, a whole new world opens up for you. Elevate every snacking or dipping experience with a platter of homemade crackers. If you've ever made biscuits, they come together just as easily. Switch up the seasonings to pair with whatever else you're serving.

2 cups all-purpose flour

1 teaspoon kosher salt, plus more for sprinkling

1 teaspoon ground black pepper, plus more for sprinkling

2 teaspoons granulated sugar

1 tablespoon grated lemon zest

2 tablespoons (1 ounce) unsalted butter, cold and cubed

¾ cup whole milk

1. Position two oven racks in the top and bottom thirds of the oven and heat the oven to 350°F. Line two rimmed baking sheets with parchment paper or silicone baking mats.

2. In a medium bowl, whisk together the flour, salt, pepper, sugar, and lemon zest.

3. Add the cubed butter. Pinch and push the small pieces of butter into the flour mixture until it forms a sandy consistency.

4. Make a well in the center of the mixture and pour in the milk. Mix the milk in with your fingertips and fold just until a dough forms. Take care to not overmix.

5. Dust your work surface with flour and turn the dough out onto the surface. Roll the dough into a large, very thin rectangle, a touch thinner than you'd roll pie dough. Cut the dough with a floured chef's knife into rectangles, squares, or strips and place on the lined baking sheets. The dough can only be rolled once, so bake off any odd bits as well for snacks. Sprinkle the dough with salt and pepper to taste.

6. Bake, rotating the pans front to back halfway through, until the edges of the crackers just start to brown, 10 to 15 minutes. If you prefer a very crisp, crunchy cracker, let your crackers bake a few minutes longer, until golden brown.

7. Crackers are best shortly after baking, but can be stored in an airtight container at room temperature for up to 3 days.

These crackers were born from an old-school entertaining recipe in which Club crackers are topped with bacon and brown sugar, then popped under the broiler for a few minutes. Don't get me wrong—they are *delicious*. I simply prefer to take the longer, even more delicious route, with better-quality ingredients. You must use real maple syrup; there is no other way. Pair these crackers with an aged cheddar and your party will be poppin'.

- 2 cups all-purpose flour
- 1 teaspoon kosher salt, plus more for sprinkling
- 1 teaspoon ground black pepper, plus more for sprinkling
- ¼ cup crumbled cooked bacon
- 2 tablespoons (1 ounce) unsalted butter, cold and cubed
- 2 teaspoons pure maple syrup, plus more for brushing
- ¾ cup whole milk

1. Position two oven racks in the top and bottom thirds of the oven and heat the oven to 350°F. Line two rimmed baking sheets with parchment paper or silicone baking mats.

2. In a medium bowl, whisk together the flour, salt, pepper, and bacon crumbles.

3. Add the cubed butter and maple syrup. Pinch and push the small pieces of butter into the flour mixture until it forms a sandy consistency.

4. Make a well in the center of the mixture and pour in the milk. Mix the milk in with your fingertips and fold just until a dough forms. Take care to not overmix.

5. Dust your work surface with flour and turn the dough out onto the surface. Roll the dough into a large rectangle about ⅛ inch thick, dusting the surface with flour as needed. Cut the dough with a floured chef's knife into rectangles, squares, or strips and place on the lined baking sheet. The dough can only be rolled once, so bake off any odd bits as well for snacks. Brush each cracker with maple syrup and sprinkle with salt and pepper to taste.

6. Bake, rotating the pans front to back halfway through, until the edges of the crackers just start to brown, 10 to 15 minutes. If you prefer a very crisp, crunchy cracker, let your crackers bake a few minutes longer, until golden brown.

7. Crackers are best shortly after baking, but can be stored in an airtight container at room temperature for up to 3 days.

What is the difference between real and imitation maple syrup anyway? Why does imitation syrup even exist and how can it be stopped?

30 MINUTES

ROASTED-TOMATO SCONES
Makes 16 scones

These scones are the best cure for your pizza-for-breakfast craving without looking totally irresponsible at school drop-off. If you do rock a slice of cold pizza in the car, I just want you to know that's epic and you're my hero. Plan ahead for your a.m. fix by making the dough the night before, pull the scones from the fridge, and bake them off in the morning.

ROASTED TOMATOES

1 container (10.5 ounces) cherry tomatoes

Extra-virgin olive oil

Salt and ground black pepper

SCONES

4½ cups all-purpose flour

¼ cup granulated sugar

2 tablespoons baking powder

1 teaspoon kosher salt

½ teaspoon ground black pepper, or to taste

1 teaspoon dried thyme

1 teaspoon dried oregano

½ teaspoon freeze-dried garlic or garlic powder

3 sticks (12 ounces) unsalted butter, cold and cubed

½ cup (4 ounces) goat cheese

1 cup heavy cream, plus more for brushing

½ cup shredded Parmesan cheese, for sprinkling (optional)

1. Position two oven racks in the top and bottom thirds of the oven and heat the oven to 400°F.

2. Roast the tomatoes: Toss the cherry tomatoes onto a baking sheet and coat with olive oil. Sprinkle with salt and pepper to taste. Roast on the upper rack until the tomatoes have popped their skins and started to brown, 15 to 20 minutes. Transfer the pan to a rack to allow the tomatoes to cool while you assemble the scone dough.

3. Leave the oven on, but reduce the temperature to 350°F. Line two rimmed baking sheets with parchment paper or silicone baking mats.

4. Make the scones: In a large bowl, whisk together the flour, sugar, baking powder, salt, black pepper, thyme, oregano, and freeze-dried garlic.

5. Add the cubed butter to the bowl. Pinch and press the butter into the flour mixture until it resembles a sandy consistency.

6. Crumble the goat cheese over the mixture and toss together, keeping the crumbles intact.

7. Make a well in the center of the flour mixture and add the roasted tomatoes and heavy cream. Use your squeaky-clean hands, and a delicate touch, to fold the wet mixture into the flour until just combined.

8. Dust your work surface with flour and turn the dough out onto the surface. Press the dough into a 12 x 5-inch rectangle. Use a sharp knife or bench scraper to cut the rectangle in half in each direction. You should have four rectangles, each measuring 6 x 2½ inches. Looking at the dough with one of the long sides facing you, cut the quarters in half again. You should now have 8 squares of dough. Make diagonal cuts across the squares to cut the dough into 16 triangles.

9. Transfer the scones to the prepared baking sheets, leaving 2 to 3 inches between them. Brush the tops of the scones with heavy cream. If desired, sprinkle with the Parmesan.

10. Bake, rotating the pans front to back halfway through, until the tops have just started to brown, 12 to 14 minutes.

11. Allow the scones to cool on the pan for 10 minutes. Transfer them to a rack to continue cooling. Serve scones warm and store leftovers in an airtight container at room temperature for up to 2 days. Rewarm scones in the toaster oven.

FRENCH ONION GOUGÈRES
Makes 60 gougères

These savory little cheese puffs are the perfect marriage of appetizer highs and lows. Fancy French gougères meet American onion soup dip. Both are delicious on their own, but together they're irresistible. One of the well-known secrets of classic American home cooking is adding a packet of French onion soup mix to the slow cooker or casserole. In this recipe, I create my own version of the packet to up the onion flavor while losing the extra sodium and preservatives.

Enjoy these savory little treats anytime by making them in advance. Pop the baking sheet with the piped blobs of dough in step 6 into the freezer instead of the oven. Gather the frozen puffs and store in an airtight bag in the freezer for up to 3 months. Bake the puffs straight from the freezer as needed. Frozen puffs will need a few minutes longer in the oven, but not much longer than when they're baked fresh.

½ cup beef stock

½ cup whole milk

8 tablespoons (4 ounces) unsalted butter

¾ cup dried minced onion or onion flakes

1 tablespoon onion powder

1 teaspoon kosher salt

¼ teaspoon celery seeds

¼ teaspoon granulated sugar

¼ teaspoon ground black pepper

⅛ teaspoon paprika

1 cup all-purpose flour

4 large eggs

2½ cups grated Gruyère or cheddar cheese

1. Position two oven racks in the top and bottom thirds of the oven and heat the oven to 400°F. Line two rimmed baking sheets with parchment paper or silicone baking mats.

2. In a medium saucepan, combine the beef stock, milk, butter, dried onion, onion powder, salt, celery seeds, sugar, pepper, and paprika. Cook over medium-high heat until the butter is melted and the mixture just begins to simmer.

3. Add the flour all at once and stir using a wooden spoon or heatproof spatula. Continue stirring over medium-high heat until the mixture comes together to form a firm dough. It should ball up and no longer stick to the sides of the pot after 3 to 5 minutes.

4. Transfer the hot dough into the bowl of a stand mixer fitted with the paddle (or to a medium bowl if using an electric hand mixer) and turn the mixer on low. Steam will escape from the dough as it cools. Once the steam clears, add the eggs, one at a time, until combined.

5. Beat the mixture at medium speed until the bowl has cooled to the touch, about 3 minutes. Add 1½ cups of the cheese and mix until combined.

6. Transfer the dough to a large piping bag. Snip the tip of the piping bag to create a nickel-size opening. Pipe small blobs, about the size of large grapes, onto the prepared baking sheets spacing them about 2 inches apart. Sprinkle each of the blobs with a little of the remaining cheese.

7. Bake, rotating the pans front to back halfway through, until they're puffy and golden brown, 18 to 20 minutes.

8. Allow the gougères to cool on the pans for a few minutes before piling up on a serving platter. Gougères are best enjoyed shortly after baking, but can be stored in an airtight container at room temperature for up to 2 days and rewarmed before serving.

 Time to sashay over to the craft store or big box store to pick up a few piping bags.

CARAMELIZED ONION FOCACCIA
Makes 1 large loaf

Bread can be very intimidating, even for the experienced procrastibaker. Focaccia is a great gateway bread because it doesn't require any hand-shaping that would take me three pages to explain but five minutes to show you in person. If you don't like caramelized onions, are we even friends? I mean, skip that part and head straight to the bread, and increase the olive oil to three tablespoons.

What's the difference between kosher salt and flaky sea salt? And who decided to iodize salt, anyway?

CARAMELIZED ONION

2 tablespoons olive oil

1 tablespoon unsalted butter

1 large red onion, chopped

2 tablespoons fresh rosemary, chopped

1 tablespoon dark brown sugar

2 garlic cloves, minced

½ teaspoon kosher salt

FOCACCIA

1 cup warm water, 110°F or very warm to the touch

1 tablespoon olive oil, plus more for greasing

3 cups all-purpose flour

1½ teaspoons kosher salt

2 teaspoons instant yeast

Flaky sea salt

1. Make the caramelized onion: In a large saucepan, combine the 2 tablespoons oil and the butter and heat over medium heat until the butter has melted. Add the onion, rosemary, and brown sugar and cook, stirring occasionally, until the onion is soft and translucent, about 10 minutes.

2. Reduce the heat to medium-low and continue cooking until the onions deepen in color, stirring occasionally, 15 to 20 minutes. Add a splash of water to the pan if it seems like they're getting dry or starting to burn.

3. Add the garlic and the ½ teaspoon kosher salt to the pan and cook, stirring, for 2 to 3 minutes more until the garlic is softened and fragrant. Remove from the heat to cool while you make the dough. (The onions can be made up to 1 week in advance and stored in an airtight container in the fridge.)

4. Make the focaccia: In a stand mixer fitted with the paddle (or by hand in a bowl), mix together the water, 1 tablespoon oil, the flour, salt, yeast, and cooled onions on low until a dough starts to form. Beat on medium-high until the dough is smooth and elastic, about 5 minutes. Transfer the dough to an oiled bowl, cover, and rest for 1 hour 30 minutes.

5. Generously coat the bottom of a 13 x 9-inch baking dish with oil.

6. Gently move the dough to the baking dish and spread with your fingertips to fill the pan, leaving little dimples in the dough as you go. Drizzle the dough with more oil.

7. Cover the dough lightly with oiled plastic wrap and rest for another 30 minutes at room temperature.

8. Position a rack in the center of the oven and heat the oven to 450°F.

9. Remove the plastic wrap and sprinkle the focaccia with the sea salt. Bake, rotating the pan front to back halfway through, until the bread is puffy and light golden brown, 15 to 18 minutes.

10. Focaccia is best enjoyed shortly after it's baked, but can be stored in an airtight container at room temperature for up to 3 days.

MALL PRETZELS
Makes 8 pretzels

Why go all the way to the mall for a pretzel when making them at home takes longer? I just realized that you could be reading this on its fiftieth printing (hey, it could happen) one hundred years from now and have no idea what a mall is. Fingers crossed you're still eating pretzels, though, because little in the world is better than a salty, buttery, hot pretzel fresh from the oven.

2½ cups all-purpose flour

1 cup water

1 tablespoon active dry yeast

2 teaspoons granulated sugar

1 teaspoon kosher salt

2 tablespoons baking soda

Pretzel salt or coarse salt, for topping

8 tablespoons (4 ounces) unsalted butter, melted

1. In a stand mixer fitted with the paddle (or in a large bowl if using an electric hand mixer), mix the flour, water, yeast, sugar, and kosher salt on low until just combined, then turn the mixer up to medium and beat for 5 minutes. Cover the bowl with a kitchen towel or plastic wrap and let rest 30 minutes.

2. Position a rack in the center of the oven and heat the oven to 425°F. Line two rimmed baking sheets with greased parchment paper or silicone baking mats. Line a cooling rack with paper towels.

3. Fill a medium saucepan with about 2 inches of water. Add the baking soda and bring to a gentle boil over medium-high heat. Reduce the heat to low.

4. Turn the dough out onto a floured work surface and divide into 8 pieces. Cover with a kitchen towel and let rest for 5 minutes.

5. Roll each piece into a long, thin snake, about 18 inches long. Roll a longer snake for large skinny pretzels and a shorter one for smaller, thicker pretzels. Twist into a pretzel shape and set on the floured cutting board. Repeat with the rest of the pretzels.

6. Place a pretzel in the water, top side down, for about 1 minute. Carefully flip the pretzel over with a fish spatula and let sit for another minute. Remove from the water with the fish spatula and set on the lined cooling rack to drain. Continue with three more pretzels.

7. Transfer the four dipped pretzels to one of the lined baking sheets and sprinkle with pretzel salt.

8. Bake, rotating the pan front to back halfway through, until the pretzels are deep golden brown, 8 to 10 minutes. Brush the pretzels with melted butter immediately after pulling them from the oven. Repeat the dipping, baking, and buttering process with the other four pretzels while the first pan is baking.

9. Allow the pretzels to cool on the pans for about 10 minutes before transferring to a rack.

10. Pretzels are best enjoyed shortly after baking, but can be stored in an airtight container at room temperature overnight. Rewarm in the toaster oven.

You definitely need good mustard to enjoy with pretzels. Maybe a few different flavors and some cheese sauce.

Those Mall Pretzels (page 164) you're baking are making you thirsty! Take a break while you bake and make your way to the tall beverage at the end of this maze. Or make your way to the fridge for a real one. Whatever. Do you.

START

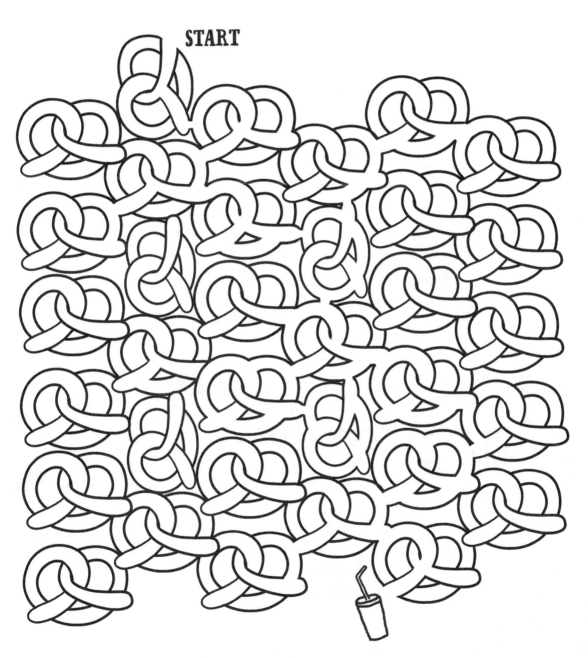

CHAPTER 9:

This May Take Awhile: Procrasti-Masterpieces

IF YOU WERE A TYPE OF CAKE, WHAT KIND OF CAKE WOULD YOU BE?

CASH IN THAT VACATION TIME, UNPLUG THE PHONE, AND DROP THE KIDS OFF AT GRANDMA'S, BECAUSE IT'S TIME TO BAKE AND THIS IS GOING TO TAKE AWHILE!

These projects are here for you when you want to dive deep, far away from the demands of daily life. When you come to and decide to resurface, you'll have a stunning masterpiece to share with the world.

MOCHA BROWNIE CHEESECAKE

Serves 10 to 12

I don't drink coffee. My husband doesn't drink coffee. Weirdos, I know. The one coffee-related drink my husband does enjoy from time to time is a mocha, because it's essentially chocolate milk spiked with just a small amount of espresso. As a family we've taken to calling his weekend mocha habit "Daddy's fancy drink." This creamy, chocolaty, espresso-spiked, fancy cheesecake is in honor of that beverage. Omit the walnuts if you're not a fan, but I think they add nice texture to the otherwise soft brownie base. If baking a cheesecake on anything other than a graham cracker crust is new to you, then welcome. It's a delicious place to be.

What other cookie, brownie, or bar could magically become a cheesecake base?

BROWNIE BOTTOM

½ cup vegetable oil

¾ cup Dutch-process cocoa powder

1¼ cups sugar

½ teaspoon kosher salt

½ teaspoon pure vanilla extract

2 large eggs

1 cup toasted walnuts, chopped

¾ cup all-purpose flour

ESPRESSO CHEESECAKE

2 pounds cream cheese, at room temperature

1 cup granulated sugar

2 tablespoons instant espresso powder

1 teaspoon pure vanilla extract

½ teaspoon kosher salt

4 large eggs

2 tablespoons all-purpose flour

Chocolate shavings (optional)

Whipped cream (optional)

1. Position a rack in the center of the oven and heat the oven to 325°F. Line a 9 x 2-inch round cake pan with enough foil to cover the bottom and up over the sides. Spray the foil.

2. Make the brownie bottom: In a small bowl or glass measuring cup, whisk together the oil, cocoa powder, sugar, salt, vanilla, and eggs. Add the walnuts and flour and stir to combine. Pour the batter into the prepared pan.

3. Bake, rotating the pan front to back halfway through, until the brownie is set, 15 to 20 minutes. Transfer the pan to a rack to cool.

4. Leave the oven on but reduce the temperature to 300°F.

5. Make the espresso cheesecake: In a stand mixer fitted with the paddle, beat the cream cheese, sugar, espresso powder, vanilla, and salt on medium-high speed, stopping to scrape down the sides of the bowl to make sure there are no cream cheese lumps, until smooth, 3 to 5 minutes.

6. With the mixer on low, add the eggs, one at a time, stopping occasionally to scrape down the sides of the bowl. Add the flour and mix to combine.

7. Pour the batter over the brownie. Gently tap the pan against your work surface to release any air bubbles. Place the pan in a larger baking dish, then onto a pulled-out oven rack. Fill the larger baking dish with about 1 inch of water.

8. Bake until the top has lost its raw sheen but the center still has a little jiggle under the surface when you move the pan, 45 to 55 minutes, starting to check for doneness around the 40-minute mark.

9. Pull out the oven rack and lift the pan from the baking dish. Transfer the cheesecake to a rack to cool. (Pull the baking dish and dump out the water.) When the pan is cool enough to handle, transfer the cheesecake to the fridge and chill for 4 hours, or up to overnight, before serving.

10. Carefully lift the cheesecake from the pan by pulling up on the foil overhang. Peel the foil away and carefully slide the cake onto a serving platter. Garnish with chocolate shavings and whipped cream, if using. Slice with a warm knife and wipe the blade down between cuts. Store leftovers, wrapped, in the fridge for up to 1 week.

THEY SAY IT'S YOUR BIRTHDAY CAKE

Serves 10 to 12

They say it's your birthday, but is it? Does it matter? It's somebody's birthday somewhere, so let's celebrate with this classic yellow sprinkle layer cake filled with chocolaty fudge frosting. This is a great entry-level layer cake if you've never made one before. Chocolate fudge frosting covers all errors. The cake recipe makes two scrumptious 8-inch round cakes, but you can also use the batter to make three 6-inch round cakes or 24 cupcakes.

CAKE

3 cups cake flour

1½ teaspoons baking powder

½ teaspoon baking soda

1 teaspoon kosher salt

¾ cup rainbow sprinkles

1½ cups buttermilk

1½ cups granulated sugar

½ cup vegetable oil

2 large eggs

2 large egg yolks

1 tablespoon pure vanilla extract

CHOCOLATE FUDGE FROSTING

2 sticks (8 ounces) unsalted butter, at room temperature

⅔ cup hot water

1 cup Dutch-process cocoa powder

8 cups powdered sugar

1 teaspoon pure vanilla extract

½ teaspoon kosher salt

Rainbow sprinkles, for topping

1. Position a rack in the center of the oven and heat the oven to 350°F. Grease and flour two 8 x 3-inch round cake pans.

2. Make the cake: In a large bowl, whisk together the cake flour, baking powder, baking soda, salt, and sprinkles.

3. In a smaller bowl or large glass measuring cup, whisk together the buttermilk, granulated sugar, oil, eggs, egg yolks, and vanilla.

4. Pour the wet ingredients into the dry and fold to combine.

5. Divide the batter evenly between the two prepared pans.

6. Bake, rotating the pans front to back halfway through baking, until the edges pull away from the pan, the cake springs back to the touch, and a toothpick inserted in the center comes out clean or with a few crumbs clinging to it, 25 to 30 minutes.

7. Transfer the pans to a rack to cool. When the pans are cool enough to handle, turn the cakes out onto a plate or clean countertop to finish cooling. Cool completely before filling or storing.

8. Make the frosting: In a stand mixer fitted with the paddle (or in a large bowl if using an electric hand mixer), beat the butter on medium-high speed, stopping to scrape down the sides of the bowl, until smooth, about 3 minutes.

9. In a small bowl or large glass measuring cup, whisk together the hot water and cocoa powder.

10. With the mixer on low, add the cocoa liquid, powdered sugar, vanilla, and salt and mix until combined. Stop and scrape down the sides of the bowl. Turn the mixer to medium-high speed and beat until all of the ingredients are

fully incorporated and the frosting is thick and creamy, 2 to 3 minutes. Let the frosting sit at room temperature for 15 to 20 minutes to thicken and cool.

11. Assemble the cake: Trim the domed tops off the cake layers and discard, or nibble on them as you work.

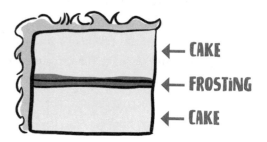

← CAKE
← FROSTING
← CAKE

12. Adhere one of the cake layers to your stand or platter with a dab of frosting. Spread one-third of the frosting over the first layer and top with the second layer. Spread a crumb coat of frosting all over the sides and top of the cake. A crumb coat consists of a thin layer of frosting meant to trap cake crumbs from infiltrating your pretty final coat. Chill the cake for 10 to 15 minutes, up to overnight, until the crumb coat and filling have set.

13. Swish swoopy swirls of frosting all over the cake using an offset spatula or the back of a spoon. Finish with sprinkles.

14. Serve the cake at room temperature. Slice with a warm knife and wipe the blade down between cuts.

15. Store leftovers, wrapped, at room temperature overnight, or in the fridge for up to 3 days.

BUTTERED PECAN ICE CREAM SANDWICHES

Makes 18 sandwiches

1 HOUR
30+
MINUTES

I'm all for making all things from scratch . . . except ice cream. Procrastibaking is supposed to be a relaxing, enjoyable activity. Listening to an ice cream machine run is like listening to rocks and screws tumble in the dryer. It's not fun. I'm fairly certain Martha Stewart was the first to publish a no-churn ice cream recipe. If you've never made it before, it's a revelation: two basic ingredients and no machine needed. So, thank you, Martha. My ears thank you too.

BUTTERED PECANS

2 cups chopped pecans

8 tablespoons (4 ounces) unsalted butter

1 teaspoon kosher salt

ICE CREAM

2 cups heavy cream

1 teaspoon pure vanilla extract

1 can (14 ounces) sweetened condensed milk

1 tablespoon molasses

COOKIES

1½ sticks (6 ounces) unsalted butter, cut into cubes, at room temperature

1½ cups dark brown sugar

2 tablespoons cornstarch

¾ teaspoon baking powder

½ teaspoon baking soda

1 teaspoon kosher salt

1 teaspoon pure vanilla extract

1 large egg

2 cups all-purpose flour

GLAZE

10 ounces bittersweet chocolate

3 tablespoons coconut oil

1. Make the buttered pecans: Position a rack in the center of the oven and heat the oven to 350°F. Line a rimmed baking sheet with parchment paper or a silicone baking mat.

2. Spread the pecans on one of the baking sheets and toast until fragrant, 5 to 10 minutes.

3. Pour the warm pecans into a small bowl. Add the butter and salt and toss together. The warm pecans will melt the butter as you toss them together. Pour them back onto the baking sheet and let the nuts sit out at room temperature while they soak up the butter. Set aside half of the pecans for the ice cream and the other half for the cookies.

4. Make the ice cream: In a stand mixer fitted with the whisk (or in a large bowl if using an electric hand mixer), whip the cream and vanilla to stiff peaks.

5. In a medium bowl, combine the condensed milk, molasses, and half of the pecans. Stir in a scoop of the whipped cream to lighten the mixture. Add the rest of the whipped cream to the bowl and gently fold together. Pour the ice cream into a storage container and freeze for 4 hours before using.

6. Position two oven racks in the top and bottom thirds of the oven and heat the oven to 350°F. Line two rimmed baking sheets with parchment paper or silicone baking mats.

7. Make the cookies: In a stand mixer fitted with the paddle (or in a large bowl if using an electric hand mixer), beat the butter, brown sugar, cornstarch, baking powder, baking soda, salt, and vanilla until light and fluffy, 3 to 5 minutes, stopping occasionally to scrape down the sides of the bowl with a rubber spatula.

8. Add the egg and mix until combined, stopping to scrape down the sides of the bowl.

9. With the mixer on low, add the flour and mix until the dough is crumbly and still a little powdery. Add half of the buttered pecans and mix to combine.

10. Scoop the dough into 1½-inch balls (0.75-ounce scoop or 1½ tablespoons). Arrange on a prepared baking sheet spaced 2 to 3 inches apart in five rows, alternating three across and two across—a 3-2-3-2-3 pattern—to ensure they bake evenly.

11. Bake, rotating the baking sheets front to back halfway through, until the cookies just start to brown around the edges, about 9 minutes.

12. Allow the cookies to cool on the baking sheets before transferring to a rack to cool. Cookies can be made up to 2 days in advance and stored in an airtight container at room temperature.

13. Make the sandwiches: Sandwich together two of the cookies with a ¼-cup scoop of the ice cream. Store the sandwiches in a zip-top bag in the freezer.

14. Make the glaze: Melt the chocolate and oil in a heatproof bowl set over a pan of simmering water (or in the microwave on high in 25-second intervals, stirring after each, about 1 minute total).

15. Dip each sandwich halfway into the melted chocolate, as if you were dunking a cookie into milk. Shake off the excess chocolate and set on a lined sheet pan. Repeat with the rest of the sandwiches. Freeze on the baking sheet for a few minutes to set the glaze.

16. Store the sandwiches, individually wrapped, in the freezer for up to 3 months.

BAKED ALASKA ICE CREAM CONES

Makes 12 cones

This is the most fun way you can serve a baked Alaska. Trust me—I served hundreds in my days as the pastry chef at Boston's (sadly, now closed) Locke-Ober restaurant. It was the second-oldest continuously run restaurant in the country, with all the Old World trimmings you could imagine. Baked Alaska had appeared on the dessert menu four times longer than I had been alive, so it was basically my job to just not screw it up. This version of that iconic dessert is far more playful in nature and doesn't require a tableside flambé.

BLACKBERRY ICE CREAM

24 ounces blackberries

¼ cup granulated sugar

1 tablespoon lemon juice

2 cups heavy cream

1 can (14 ounces) sweetened condensed milk

1 teaspoon pure vanilla extract

VANILLA ICE CREAM

2 cups heavy cream

1 teaspoon pure vanilla extract

1 can (14 ounces) sweetened condensed milk

ICE CREAM CONE CUPCAKES

12 flat-bottomed wafer ice cream cones

1½ cups cake flour

¼ cup rainbow sprinkles

¾ teaspoon baking powder

¼ teaspoon baking soda

½ teaspoon kosher salt

¾ cup granulated sugar

¼ cup buttermilk

¼ cup whole milk

¼ cup vegetable oil

2 large eggs

1½ teaspoons pure vanilla extract

MERINGUE

1 cup granulated sugar

⅓ cup water

4 large egg whites

Pinch of kosher salt

½ teaspoon cream of tartar

1. Make the blackberry ice cream: In a large saucepan, combine the blackberries, sugar, and lemon juice and cook over medium-high heat, stirring occasionally, until the berries soften and some of the water evaporates, about 5 minutes. Remove from the heat and puree the mixture with a stick blender (or pour into a traditional blender) and pulse to puree. Strain the puree through a fine-mesh sieve into a large bowl.

2. In a stand mixer fitted with the whisk (or in a large bowl if using an electric hand mixer), whip the heavy cream to stiff peaks.

3. Add the condensed milk and vanilla to the blackberry puree and whisk to combine. Stir in a scoop of the whipped cream to lighten the mixture. Add the rest of the whipped cream to the bowl and gently fold together until completely combined. Pour the ice cream into a 1-quart storage container and freeze for at least 4 hours before using.

4. Make the vanilla ice cream: In a stand mixer fitted with the whisk (or in a large bowl if using an electric hand mixer), whip the cream and vanilla to stiff peaks.

5. Pour the condensed milk into a large bowl. Stir in a scoop of the whipped cream to lighten the milk. Add the rest of the whipped cream to the bowl and gently fold together until completely combined. Pour the ice cream into a 1-quart storage container and freeze for at least 4 hours before using.

6. Make the ice cream cone cupcakes: Position a rack in the center of the oven and heat the oven to 350°F. Stand the ice cream cones up in the cups of a muffin pan.

7. In a large bowl, whisk together the cake flour, sprinkles, baking powder, baking soda, and salt.

8. In a smaller bowl or large glass measuring cup, whisk together the sugar, buttermilk, whole milk, oil, eggs, and vanilla.

9. Pour the wet ingredients into the dry and fold to combine.

10. Fill the base of the cones with batter and stop before the wide part of the cone.

11. Bake, carefully rotating the pan front to back halfway through, until the cupcakes have domed and spring back to the touch, 8 to 10 minutes.

12. Allow the cupcakes to cool in the pan for a few minutes before moving to a rack to finish cooling. Cool completely before filling.

13. Top each of the cupcakes with a small scoop of vanilla ice cream, just filling the wide part of the cones. Top the vanilla ice cream with a standard scoop of the blackberry ice cream. Stand the cones up in the freezer until the ice cream has completely firmed up. At this point you can wrap the cones individually and freeze for up to 3 days.

14. Shortly before serving, make the meringue: In a small saucepan, combine the sugar and water and cook over medium-high heat until it reaches the soft-ball stage, 235°F on a candy thermometer.

15. In a stand mixer fitted with the whisk attachment (or in a large bowl if using an electric hand mixer), combine the egg whites, salt, and cream of tartar and whisk on low speed to break up the whites. Increase the speed to medium-high and whip until soft peaks form, 5 to 8 minutes. Turn the speed back down to low and slowly pour in the hot sugar in a steady stream. Bring the speed back up to medium-high and whip for a few more minutes, until the meringue is stiff and glossy.

16. Add the meringue to a piping bag fitted with a large star tip. Pipe little stars all over the ice cream so that none shows through. Return the piped cones to the freezer as you work to finish the others.

17. Topped cones can be frozen up to 4 hours before toasting the meringue with a kitchen torch and serving.

Why is it called Baked Alaska? Why not Baked Wyoming?

BANANA SPLIT CREPE CAKE
Serves 6 to 8

This crepe cake is bound to put a smile on the face of everyone who sees and tastes it. In this over-the-top dessert, the familiar flavors of a banana split meet the sophistication of a classic French pastry. It's the perfect cake to make for someone who doesn't like cake, but you want to make a cake for anyway.

CREPES

2 large eggs

¾ cup whole milk

½ cup water

1 cup all-purpose flour

3 tablespoons (1½ ounces) unsalted butter, melted

2½ tablespoons granulated sugar

1 teaspoon pure vanilla extract

¼ teaspoon kosher salt

PASTRY CREAM

6 large egg yolks

1 banana, mashed

⅔ cup granulated sugar

3 tablespoons cornstarch

Pinch of kosher salt

2 cups whole milk

1 tablespoon unsalted butter

1 tablespoon pure vanilla extract

BUTTERCREAM

¼ cup pasteurized egg whites, or 4 large egg whites

½ cup granulated sugar

¼ teaspoon kosher salt

2 sticks (8 ounces) unsalted butter, cold and cubed

1½ teaspoons pure vanilla extract

¼ cup strawberry preserves

2 ounces bittersweet chocolate, melted

HOT FUDGE

1⅓ cups heavy cream

1½ cups dark brown sugar

¼ cup light corn syrup

4 ounces dark chocolate, chopped

4 tablespoons (2 ounces) unsalted butter

¼ teaspoon kosher salt

1 tablespoon pure vanilla extract

TOPPING

1 medium banana

Whipped cream

½ cup chopped toasted walnuts

Maraschino cherry

1. Make the crepes: In a medium bowl, combine the eggs, milk, water, flour, melted butter, granulated sugar, vanilla, and salt and whisk until smooth. Chill the batter in an airtight container for at least 1 hour, or up to overnight, before using.

2. Line a rimmed baking sheet with foil and keep the box of foil nearby.

3. Warm a small nonstick omelet pan over medium-low heat. Ladle 2 to 3 tablespoons of crepe batter into the center of the pan and swirl the pan to spread the batter out to the edges. Cook until the edges just start to brown, 1 to 2 minutes. Use a fish spatula to flip the crepe. Cook on the other side for just a minute. Slide the crepe onto the foil-lined sheet. Return the pan to the heat and make another crepe. Slide that crepe onto the foil next to the first one you made. Top the pair with another piece of foil. Continue making crepes, wiping out the pan as needed with a paper towel, and layering foil between them, until the batter is gone. You should get 20 to 25 crepes from the batter. Store the crepes, wrapped, at room temperature for a few hours, or in the fridge overnight. (The crepes can be made a day in advance.)

4. Make the pastry cream: In a large heatproof bowl, whisk together the egg yolks, mashed banana, granulated sugar, cornstarch, and salt.

5. In a saucepan, bring the milk to a boil over medium-high heat. Remove from the heat. Slowly whisk half of the hot milk into the egg mixture, whisking vigorously to combine. Pour the tempered egg mixture back into the saucepan of hot milk.

6. Cook over medium-low heat, stirring constantly with a heatproof silicone spatula, until thickened to the texture of mayonnaise, about 5 minutes.

7. Strain the pastry cream through a fine-mesh strainer into a medium bowl. Whisk in the butter and vanilla.

8. Press plastic wrap against the surface of the pastry cream to prevent it from forming a skin and store in the fridge for up to 3 days.

9. Make the buttercream: In a medium microwave-safe bowl, whisk together the egg whites, granulated sugar, and salt. Heat the mixture in the microwave on high for 1 minute at a time, whisking after each interval, until the sugar has dissolved, 2 to 3 minutes. (Alternatively, heat the mixture in a heatproof bowl set over a pan of simmering water, whisking occasionally, until the sugar has dissolved.) If you're using fresh egg whites, heat the mixture until it registers 160°F on a candy thermometer.

10. Pour the egg white mixture into the bowl of a stand mixer fitted with the whisk (or in a large bowl if using an electric hand mixer). Whip the egg whites on low speed just until the mixture starts to loosen and foam. Turn the mixer up to high speed and beat the egg whites until it resembles a white, fluffy cloud, 8 to 10 minutes.

11. Turn the mixer down to low speed and add the butter, a few cubes at a time. The mixture will appear curdled, but that's okay. Once all the butter has been added, turn the mixer up to medium-high speed and whip until the buttercream is smooth, glossy, and light in color, 8 to 10 minutes. Add the vanilla and mix to combine. Divide the buttercream into thirds. Fold the strawberry preserves into one-third, the melted chocolate into another, and leave the third one plain. Chill all three, covered, in the fridge for 30 minutes, or up to overnight.

12. Make the hot fudge: In a medium saucepan, combine the heavy cream, brown sugar, and corn syrup. Cook over medium heat, stirring occasionally, until the sugar melts.

13. Whisk in the chopped chocolate, butter, and salt until the chocolate and butter have melted. Cook the mixture, stirring, until it just starts to simmer, 3 to 5 minutes more.

14. Remove the pan from the heat and stir in the vanilla. Use the hot fudge sauce immediately, or store in an airtight container in the fridge for up to 1 week.

15. If made ahead and refrigerated, rewarm the chilled hot fudge sauce in the microwave for 30-second increments, stirring after each one, or in a small saucepan over low heat, stirring until your desired consistency is achieved.

16. Build the cake: Secure one of the crepes on your serving platter with a dab of pastry cream. Spread 1 to 2 tablespoons pastry cream onto the crepe using an offset spatula. Top with another crepe and repeat with the pastry cream. Continue until all of the crepes have been layered.

17. Use an ice cream scoop dipped in warm water to scoop the vanilla buttercream and place the scoop on top of the crepe cake. Rinse the scoop and repeat with the other two flavors. Chill for 30 minutes to 1 hour, until the buttercream is firm and the crepe cake is set.

18. For the topping: Right before serving, halve the banana lengthwise. Dry the cut sides of the banana with a paper towel and stick onto either side of the buttercream scoops. Drizzle the faux sundae with warm fudge sauce. Pipe or dollop whipped cream onto the buttercream scoops and sprinkle with walnuts. Complete with a cherry on top and serve immediately.

19. Slice with a warm knife and wipe down the blade between cuts. To store leftovers, remove any leftover banana and enjoy it as a snack (it'll just brown while stored) and store in an airtight container in the fridge overnight.

RAINBOW ROLL CAKE

Serves 6 to 8

Adding rainbow colors to this cake doesn't change the flavor, but it sure does make it fun to look at! Using gel food coloring ensures bold colors without watering down the batter. Customize the shades to match a party theme, current holiday, or birthday person's favorite colors.

CAKE

2½ cups cake flour

1 teaspoon baking powder

¼ teaspoon baking soda

1 teaspoon kosher salt

6 large eggs, separated

1½ cups granulated sugar

¾ cup vegetable oil

2 teaspoons pure vanilla extract

½ cup buttermilk

Gel food coloring in pink, orange, yellow, green, blue, and purple

Powdered sugar, for dusting

FILLING

8 tablespoons (4 ounces) unsalted butter, at room temperature

8 tablespoons (4 ounces) vegetable shortening

2 teaspoons pure vanilla extract

⅛ teaspoon kosher salt

3½ cups powdered sugar

2 tablespoons whole milk

1. Position a rack in the center of the oven and heat the oven to 350°F. Line a rimmed baking sheet with parchment paper. Grease the pan before placing the parchment to make it stick to the pan. Grease the parchment and sides of the pan.

2. Make the cake: In a large bowl, whisk together the flour, baking powder, baking soda, and salt.

3. In a medium bowl, whisk together the egg yolks, granulated sugar, oil, vanilla, and buttermilk.

4. In a stand mixer fitted with the whisk (or in a metal bowl if using an electric hand mixer), whip the egg whites on medium-high speed until stiff peaks form, 2 to 3 minutes.

5. Pour the egg yolk/butter mixture into the flour mixture and whisk to combine.

6. Switch to a rubber spatula and gently fold the egg whites into the cake batter in three additions.

7. Divide the batter evenly among six bowls and tint each of the bowls of batter a different color of the rainbow using the gel food colorings. Pour each color of batter into a separate piping bag and snip the tip to create a dime-size opening. Pipe diagonal stripes of batter in rainbow order (pink, orange, yellow, green, blue, purple) into the prepared pan. If straight lines aren't your thing (or you don't have piping bags), scoop dots of each color in random spots throughout the pan.

8. Bake, rotating the pan halfway through, until the edges pull away from the pan and the cake springs back to the touch, 10 to 12 minutes.

9. Spread a clean kitchen towel out on your work surface and dust with powdered sugar. Immediately after pulling the cake from the oven, run a knife along all the edges of the pan and confidently flip the cake out onto the towel. Peel off the parchment. Starting at one of the short ends, roll the cake up into the towel. Allow the cake to cool, wrapped in the towel, for 30 minutes.

10. Make the filling: In a stand mixer fitted with the paddle (or in a large bowl if using an electric hand mixer), beat the butter until smooth and no small lumps remain, 2 to 3 minutes. Scrape down the sides of the bowl and add the vegetable shortening, vanilla, and salt. Beat until the mixture is fluffy and lighter in color, stopping to scrape down the sides of the bowl, 3 to 5 minutes.

11. Turn the mixer to low speed and slowly add the powdered sugar until just combined. Stop and scrape down the sides of the bowl, then turn the mixer up to medium and beat until the mixture is bright white and fluffy, 3 to 5 minutes.

12. With the mixer on low speed, add the milk, 1 tablespoon at a time, until combined.

13. Carefully unroll the cake from the towel. Spread the filling over the cake with an offset spatula. Use the cake's "muscle memory" to roll back up. Slide the cake onto a platter and chill for at least 30 minutes, or up to overnight covered in the fridge.

14. Slice with a warm serrated knife, wiping the blade clean between cuts.

15. Store leftovers, wrapped, in the fridge for up to 3 days.

SNOWBALL CAKE

Serves 6 to 8

I think every baker loves reinventing childhood classics, and I'm no exception to the rule. I didn't mess with any of the flavors here; I just made my snowball from scratch with quality ingredients. The catch: It's enormous! This whimsical play on scale would make for an ah-mazing birthday cake or everyday celebration cake. Customize the color of the coconut to the guest of honor's favorite color.

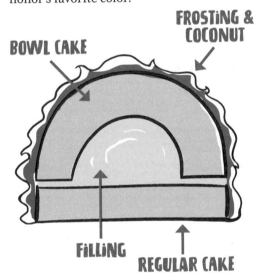

FROSTING & COCONUT

BOWL CAKE

FILLING

REGULAR CAKE

CAKE

1½ cups all-purpose flour

1 cup granulated sugar

¾ cup Dutch-process cocoa powder

1½ teaspoons baking soda

1 teaspoon baking powder

1 teaspoon kosher salt

¾ cup water

¾ cup whole milk

1 teaspoon white vinegar

1 teaspoon pure vanilla extract

3 tablespoons vegetable oil

2 large eggs

COATING

2 cups sweetened shredded coconut

Pink gel food coloring

MARSHMALLOW FILLING AND FROSTING

¼ cup plus 5 tablespoons water

½ teaspoon pure vanilla extract

1 tablespoon unflavored powdered gelatin

1 teaspoon light corn syrup

1 cup granulated sugar

8 tablespoons (4 ounces) unsalted butter, at room temperature

2 cups powdered sugar

1. Position a rack in the center of the oven and heat the oven to 350°F. Grease and flour a 6-inch-diameter stainless-steel bowl and a 6-inch round cake pan.

2. Make the cakes: In a large bowl, whisk together the flour, granulated sugar, cocoa powder, baking soda, baking powder, and salt.

3. In a smaller bowl or large glass measuring cup, whisk together the water, milk, vinegar, vanilla, oil, and eggs.

4. Pour the wet ingredients over the dry and whisk until just combined.

5. Add two-thirds of the batter to the bowl and one-third to the round cake pan. Set both pans on a baking sheet. Bake, rotating the pans front to back halfway through, until a toothpick inserted in the center comes out clean or with a few crumbs clinging to it, 20 to 25 minutes for the round cake and 35 to 40 minutes for the bowl cake.

6. Transfer the cakes to a rack to cool. Turn the 6-inch flat layer out onto a platter or clean countertop to continue cooling. Leave the bowl cake in the bowl to cool completely before filling, about 1 hour.

7. Use a spoon to scoop out the middle of the bowl cake, leaving about 1½ inches of cake all the way around the bowl. Level off the top of the flat layer. Keep the bowl cake nearby. Discard the scraps and innards or snack on them.

8. Make the coating: In a large zip-top bag, combine the coconut and a few drops of pink food coloring. Seal the bag and toss to color the coconut.

9. Make the filling and frosting: In a stand mixer fitted with the whisk, combine ¼ cup of the water, the vanilla, and gelatin.

10. In a small saucepan, combine the remaining 5 tablespoons water, the corn syrup, and granulated sugar and cook over medium-high heat until the mixture reaches soft-ball stage, 240°F on a candy thermometer.

11. Pour the hot sugar mixture into the bowl of the stand mixer. Turn the mixer on low for just a minute or so to allow the steam to dissipate from the bowl. Turn the mixer up to medium-high speed and whip until light, bright white, and fluffy, about 5 minutes.

12. Scoop half of the marshmallow filling into the middle of the bowl cake and smooth the top flat. Place the flat layer cake on top of the filling, cut side down. Turn the entire thing out onto your serving plate or platter.

13. Return the bowl with the rest of the marshmallow to the mixer and switch to the paddle.

14. Add the butter and beat on medium-high speed to combine.

15. With the mixer on low speed, slowly add the powdered sugar and mix until combined. Scrape down the sides of the bowl and fold in any remaining bits of sugar.

16. Spread the frosting all over the outside of the cake. Scoop up handfuls of the colored coconut and press it into the frosting all over the cake.

17. Serve the snowball immediately. Store leftovers, covered, at room temperature for up to 3 days.

LEMON-BERRY LAYER CAKE

Serves 6 to 10

1 HOUR
30+
MINUTES

This cake is a total celebration of summer, but since the berry flavor comes from preserves, it can, thankfully, be enjoyed year-round. I've provided instructions for assembling this cake into a towering four layers. Skip the torting step (splitting the cakes) and go with two layers if you're feeling less ambitious. Add the berry preserves below the lemon curd filling if that's the route you take.

CAKE

2⅓ cups cake flour

1 teaspoon baking powder

¼ teaspoon baking soda

1 teaspoon kosher salt

6 large eggs, separated

1½ cups granulated sugar

8 tablespoons (4 ounces) unsalted butter, melted

¼ cup vegetable oil

1 tablespoon grated lemon zest

2 teaspoons pure vanilla extract

½ cup buttermilk

LEMON CURD

¾ cup lemon juice

1 large egg

3 large egg yolks

⅔ cup granulated sugar

4 tablespoons (2 ounces) unsalted butter, cubed

Pinch of kosher salt

½ teaspoon pure vanilla extract

SWISS MERINGUE BUTTERCREAM

¾ cup pasteurized egg whites, or 4 large egg whites

1¼ cups granulated sugar

½ teaspoon kosher salt

5 sticks (20 ounces) unsalted butter, cold and cubed

1 tablespoon pure vanilla extract

Yellow and purple gel food coloring

1¼ cups mixed-berry preserves

Fresh berries, for garnish

Whipped cream or vanilla ice cream, for serving

1. Position a rack in the center of the oven and heat the oven to 350°F. Spray and flour two 6 x 3–inch round cake pans.

2. Make the cake: In a large bowl, whisk together the cake flour, baking powder, baking soda, and salt.

3. In a medium bowl, whisk together the egg yolks, sugar, melted butter, oil, lemon zest, and vanilla. Whisk in the buttermilk.

4. In a stand mixer fitted with the whisk (or in a metal bowl if using an electric hand mixer), whip the egg whites on medium-high speed until stiff peaks form, 2 to 3 minutes.

5. Pour the egg yolk–butter mixture into the flour mixture and whisk to combine.

6. Switch to a rubber spatula and gently fold the egg whites into the cake batter in three additions.

7. Divide the batter evenly between the two prepared pans, but not any higher than three-quarters full. If you're using shallower cake pans, you may end up with enough batter for a third layer.

8. Bake, rotating the pans front to back halfway through, until the edges pull away from the pan, the cake springs back to the touch, and a toothpick inserted in the center comes out clean or with a few crumbs clinging to it, 25 to 30 minutes.

9. Transfer the pans to a rack to cool. When the pans are cool enough to handle, turn the cakes out onto a plate or clean countertop to finish cooling. Cool completely before filling or storing.

10. Make the curd: In a large microwave-safe bowl, whisk together the lemon juice, egg, egg yolks, sugar, butter, and salt. Microwave on high for 1 minute. Whisk to distribute the heat. Repeat the heating and whisking process four to five more times, until the mixture has thickened to the consistency of Greek yogurt. Whisk in the vanilla. The curd will continue to thicken as it cools. Press plastic against the surface of the curd and refrigerate until cool, about 20 minutes.

11. Make the Swiss meringue buttercream: In a medium microwave-safe bowl, whisk together the egg whites, sugar, and salt. Heat the mixture in the microwave on high for 1 minute at a time, whisking after each interval, until the sugar has dissolved, 2 to 3 minutes. (Alternatively, heat the mixture in a heatproof bowl set over a pan of simmering water, whisking occasionally, until the sugar has dissolved.) If you're using fresh egg whites, heat the mixture until it registers 160°F on a candy thermometer.

12. Pour the egg mixture into the bowl of a stand mixer fitted with the whisk (or in a large bowl if using an electric hand mixer). Whip the egg whites on low speed just until they start to loosen and foam. Turn the mixer up to high speed and beat the egg whites until they resemble a white, fluffy cloud, 8 to 10 minutes.

13. Turn the mixer down to low speed and add the butter, a few cubes at a time. The mixture will appear curdled, but that's okay. Once all the butter has been added, turn the mixer up to medium-high speed and whip until the buttercream is smooth, glossy, and light in color, 8 to 10 minutes. Add the vanilla until just combined.

14. Scoop ¼ cup of the buttercream into a small bowl and tint with the yellow gel coloring. Add the yellow-tinted buttercream to a small piping bag fitted with a large star tip. Fold 1 cup of the berry preserves into the remaining buttercream. Set aside the remaining preserves for the filling. Fill a piping bag with about 1 cup of the berry buttercream and snip the tip to create a dime-size opening.

15. Assemble the cake: Trim the domed tops off the cake layers and discard, or nibble on them as you work. Slice each cake in half horizontally to create four thin cake layers total.

16. Adhere one of the cake layers to your stand or platter with a dab of buttercream. Spread a thin layer of berry buttercream over the surface of the cake layer using an offset spatula. Spread half of the remaining berry preserves on top of that. Spread a 1-inch-thick layer of berry buttercream on top of the preserves and top with a second cake layer. Press down gently to adhere. Spread a thin layer of berry buttercream over the second layer. Use the piping bag of berry buttercream to pipe a ring around the outer edges of the cake layer to create a retaining wall for the lemon curd filling. Spread about 1 cup of the lemon curd within the buttercream ring and reserve the remaining curd for serving. Top with a third cake layer, pressing down gently around the edges to adhere the cake to the ring of buttercream. Spread a thin layer of berry buttercream over the surface of the third layer using an offset spatula. Spread the remaining berry preserves on top of that. Spread a 1-inch-thick layer of berry buttercream on top of the preserves and top with the final cake layer. If at any point your cake starts to feel soft or wobbly, pop it in the fridge until it's firm enough to work with. Spread a thin crumb coat of buttercream all over the sides and top of the cake. Chill the cake for 1 hour, or up to overnight, until the crumb coat and fillings have set.

17. Place the crumb-coated cake on a turntable. Reserve 1 cup of the buttercream for decorating the top and spread the rest over the sides and top of the cake using an offset spatula. Smooth the sides of the cake with a warm bench scraper or large icing spatula.

18. Divide the reserved 1 cup berry buttercream in half and tint one half with purple gel coloring. Fill each of two small piping bags fitted with large star tips with the berry buttercream and the purple buttercream. Use all three piping bags to pipe three shades of swirls and kisses all around the top of the cake. Garnish with fresh berries, if available.

19. Serve the cake at room temperature with the remaining lemon curd, whipped cream, ice cream, or more fresh berries. Slice with a warm knife and wipe the blade down between cuts.

20. Store leftovers, wrapped, in the fridge for up to 3 days.

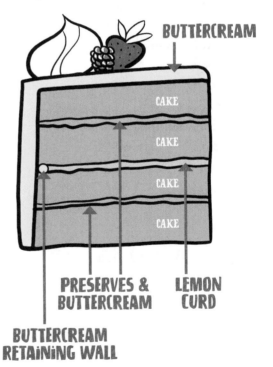

BUTTERCREAM

CAKE

CAKE

CAKE

CAKE

PRESERVES & BUTTERCREAM

LEMON CURD

BUTTERCREAM RETAINING WALL

TURTLE LAYER CAKE
Serves 6 to 10

This layer cake may seem elaborate, but all of the components can be made days before assembling. It's a great project for taking up pockets of time throughout a tedious workweek, with the grand finale assembly occurring right before you blast off for the weekend. It's Friday, and I'm in love with a turtle cake.

CHOCOLATE CAKE

8 tablespoons (4 ounces) unsalted butter, at room temperature

1½ cups dark brown sugar

1 cup granulated sugar

1 teaspoon baking soda

1 teaspoon kosher salt

4 large eggs

1 cup Dutch-process cocoa powder

1 cup warm water

½ cup whole milk

2 cups all-purpose flour

CANDIED PECANS

1 large egg white

2 cups chopped pecans

½ cup granulated sugar

½ teaspoon kosher salt

CARAMEL SAUCE

¾ cup granulated sugar

¼ cup water

Pinch of cream of tartar

½ teaspoon kosher salt

¼ cup heavy cream

3 tablespoons (1½ ounces) unsalted butter

½ teaspoon pure vanilla extract

BUTTERCREAM FROSTING

2 sticks (8 ounces) unsalted butter, at room temperature

1 cup (8 ounces) vegetable shortening (or more butter)

1 tablespoon pure vanilla extract

¼ teaspoon kosher salt

1 bag (2 pounds) powdered sugar (7½ cups)

GANACHE

6 ounces bittersweet chocolate, chopped

⅔ cup heavy cream

Turtle candies (optional)

1. Position a rack in the center of the oven and heat the oven to 350°F. Grease and flour two 6 x 3-inch round cake pans.

2. Make the chocolate cake: In a stand mixer fitted with the paddle (or in a large bowl if using an electric hand mixer), beat the butter, brown sugar, granulated sugar, baking soda, and salt on medium-high speed, stopping to scrape down the sides of the bowl to make sure there are no butter lumps, until fluffy and lighter in color, 3 to 5 minutes.

3. Add the eggs, one at a time, and mix until combined. Stop and scrape down the sides of the bowl.

4. In a small bowl or large glass measuring cup, whisk together the cocoa powder and warm water. Whisk in the milk.

5. With the mixer on low, add half the flour to the butter mixture until just incorporated. Slowly add half the chocolate mixture until combined. Stop and scrape down the sides of the bowl. Add the remaining flour and mix until combined. Add the last of the chocolate mixture and mix to combine. Stop and scrape down the sides of the bowl one last time and fold in any unincorporated ingredients by hand.

6. Divide the batter evenly between the two prepared pans, but not any higher than three-quarters full. If you're using shallower cake pans, you may end up with enough batter for a third layer.

7. Bake, rotating the pans front to back halfway through, until the edges pull away from the pan, the cake springs back to the touch, and a toothpick inserted in the center comes out clean or with a few crumbs clinging to it, 25 to 30 minutes.

8. Transfer the pans to a rack to cool. When the pans are cool enough to handle, turn the cakes out onto a plate or clean countertop to finish cooling. Cool completely before filling or storing.

9. Meanwhile, make the candied pecans: Line a rimmed baking sheet with parchment paper or a silicone baking mat. In a large bowl, whisk the egg white until frothy. Add the pecans, granulated sugar, and salt and stir to combine. Spread the coated nuts out on the prepared baking sheet. Bake, shaking the pan halfway through so that the nuts don't stick, until golden brown, 10 to 15 minutes.

10. Allow the nuts to cool completely before using. Store in an airtight container at room temperature for up to 2 weeks.

11. Make the caramel sauce: In a small saucepan, combine the granulated sugar, water, cream of tartar, and salt. Cook over medium-high heat without stirring until dark amber in color, about 5 minutes.

12. Remove the pan from the heat and carefully whisk in the heavy cream. The caramel will sputter and release steam as the cream is added.

13. Whisk in the butter and vanilla. Set the caramel sauce aside to cool. Caramel sauce can be made up to 3 days in advance and stored in the fridge in an airtight container.

14. Make the buttercream frosting: In a stand mixer fitted with the paddle (or in a large bowl if using an electric hand mixer), beat the butter on medium-high speed until smooth and no small lumps remain, 2 to 3 minutes. Scrape down the sides of the bowl and add the vegetable shortening, vanilla, and salt. Beat until the mixture is fluffy and lighter in color, stopping to scrape down the sides of the bowl, 3 to 5 minutes.

15. Turn the mixer to low speed and slowly add the powdered sugar until just combined. Stop and scrape down the sides of the bowl, then turn the mixer up to medium and beat until the frosting is bright white and fluffy, 3 to 5 minutes.

16. With the mixer on low speed, add ¾ cup of the cooled caramel sauce until combined.

17. Assemble the cake: Trim the domed tops off the cake layers and discard, or nibble on them as you work. Slice each cake in half horizontally to create four thin cake layers total.

18. Adhere one of your cake layers to a stand or platter with a dab of buttercream. Spread about 1 cup buttercream evenly over the cake layer. Drizzle with 1 tablespoon or so of the caramel sauce and sprinkle with 2 to 3 pinches of the candied pecans. Top with a second cake layer. Repeat layering the buttercream, drizzling the caramel, and sprinkling the candied pecans for this and the next layers. Top with the remaining cake layer. Spread a thin crumb coat of buttercream all over the sides and top of the cake. Chill the cake for 1 hour, or up to overnight, until the crumb coat and fillings have set.

19. Place the crumb-coated cake on a turntable. Reserve 1 cup of the buttercream for decorating the top and spread the rest over the sides and top of the cake using an offset spatula. Smooth the sides of the cake with a warm bench scraper or large icing spatula. Chill the cake for 10 minutes to set the buttercream.

20. Make the ganache: Add the chocolate to a small heatproof bowl. Scald the cream in a coffee cup if using the microwave or in a small saucepan over medium-high heat. Pour the cream over the chocolate and whisk to combine.

21. Spoon drips of warm ganache over the sides of the cake and fill in the top of the cake with enough ganache to cover. Smooth with an offset spatula.

22. Scoop the reserved 1 cup buttercream into a piping bag fitted with a large star tip and pipe swirls on top of the ganache around the outer edges of the cake. Sprinkle the swirls with the candied pecans and garnish with turtle candies, if using.

23. Serve the cake at room temperature with any leftover caramel, ganache, candied pecans, or turtle candies. Slice with a warm knife and wipe the blade down between cuts.

24. Store leftovers, wrapped, in the fridge for up to 3 days.

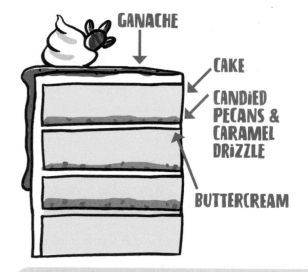

GANACHE

CAKE

CANDiED PECANS & CARAMEL DRiZZLE

BUTTERCREAM

Do you really need to? Are you all right? Well, okay. I guess you could make the turtles from scratch.

CLASSIC CROQUEMBOUCHE

Serves 6 to 8

If you're looking to create a baking masterpiece while taking up as much time as possible, there is no better cuisine to turn to than the French. Croquembouche is traditionally served as a wedding cake or celebration cake in France, and for good reason. As complex as it may appear, each of the individual tasks isn't really that daunting. Spinning sugar is intimidating at first, but once you get the hang of it you'll be topping everything with a ball of sweet gold thread.

CHOUX PUFFS

½ cup water

½ cup whole milk

8 tablespoons (4 ounces) unsalted butter

¼ teaspoon kosher salt

1 cup all-purpose flour

5 large eggs

1 teaspoon pure vanilla extract

PASTRY CREAM

6 large egg yolks

⅔ cup granulated sugar

3 tablespoons cornstarch

Pinch of kosher salt

2 cups whole milk

1 tablespoon unsalted butter

1 tablespoon pure vanilla extract

CARAMEL

1 cup granulated sugar

¼ cup water

28 x 22-inch poster board for mold

1. Position two oven racks in the top and bottom thirds of the oven and heat the oven to 350°F. Line two rimmed baking sheets with parchment paper or silicone baking mats.

2. Make the choux puffs: In a medium saucepan, combine the water, milk, butter, and salt. Cook over medium-high heat until the butter is melted and the mixture just begins to simmer.

3. Add the flour all at once and stir using a wooden spoon or heatproof spatula. Continue stirring over medium-high heat until the mixture comes together to form a firm dough. It should ball up around the spoon and no longer stick to the sides of the pot, 3 to 5 minutes.

4. Pour the hot dough into the bowl of a stand mixer fitted with the paddle (or in a medium bowl if using an electric hand mixer). Turn the mixer on low. Steam will escape from the dough as it cools. Once the steam clears, beat in the eggs, one at a time, until combined. Beat in the vanilla.

5. Beat the mixture at medium speed until the bowl has cooled to the touch, about 3 minutes.

6. Transfer the dough to a large piping bag. Snip the tip of the piping bag to create a nickel-size opening. Pipe small blobs, about the size of a large grape, onto the prepared baking sheets spaced about 2 inches apart. Bake, rotating the pans front to back halfway through, until puffed and golden brown, 10 to 15 minutes. Before baking, the piped dough can be frozen, gathered into a zip-top bag, and stored in the freezer for up to 3 months. Bake just as you'd bake fresh puffs, just for a few minutes longer.

7. Allow the puffs to cool on the pans before transferring to a rack. Puffs can be baked up to a day in advance and stored in a zip-top bag at room temperature.

8. Make the pastry cream: In a large heat-proof bowl, whisk together the egg yolks, sugar, cornstarch, and salt.

9. In a saucepan, bring the milk to a boil over medium-high heat. Remove from the heat. Slowly add half of the hot milk to the egg mixture, whisking vigorously to combine. Pour the tempered egg mixture back into the pan of hot milk.

10. Cook over medium-low heat, stirring constantly with a heatproof silicone spatula, until thickened to the texture of mayonnaise, about 5 minutes.

11. Strain the pastry cream through a fine-mesh sieve into a medium bowl. Add the butter and vanilla and mix until combined. At this point the pastry cream can be stored in an airtight container, with plastic wrap pressed against the surface, for up to 2 days in advance.

12. Fill a piping bag fitted with a small round tip with the pastry cream.

13. Poke the tip into one of the puffs and fill with pastry cream. Set the puff on a lined baking sheet. Repeat with all of the puffs and chill them while making the cone (to support the croquembouche) and the caramel.

14. To make a mold in which to build the croquembouche, roll the poster board up into a cone shape, making sure the widest part is about 8 inches in diameter. Use tape to secure the edges. Line the inside of your cone with a piece of parchment paper. Trim the pointed edges of the cone so that it sits flat. This will help when it's time to turn the croquembouche out.

15. Make the caramel: Have a large bowl or sink filled with cool water. In a medium saucepan, combine the sugar and water and cook over medium-high heat until deep amber in color, 3 to 5 minutes. Remove from the heat and dip the bottom of the pan into the cool water for just a moment to stop the caramel from cooking further. Place the pan on a trivet or folded kitchen towel for added stability and safety. Keep a bowl of cold water nearby just in case a drop of sugar gets on your skin.

16. With the pointed end of the cone down, drop a cream puff into the cone so that the bottom of the puff is facing up. Dip the side of another puff into the caramel and place it into the cone so that the caramel glues the two puffs together. Continue with more puffs, placing them into the cone so that the tops face the sides of the cone. The puffs should fit snugly into the tip of the cone and then line the sides of the cone as you work your way to the wider end. Place your cone in a vase or a tall glass if you're not comfortable holding it while working with the hot sugar. Add the last row of puffs so that the bottoms of the puffs are facing up. This will create a more stable base for the bottom of the croquembouche when you turn it out of the mold.

17. Turn the filled cone over onto your serving platter or cake stand. Lift off the poster board cone and peel off the parchment paper. Add more puffs to the base of your croquembouche if it feels lopsided to you or there are any gaps.

18. Use the remaining caramel to create a gorgeous spun-sugar garnish for your cro-quembouche. To do this, rewarm the caramel over low heat, just until it's fluid again. Lightly spray a cookie sheet with pan spray. Dip a fork into the caramel and move it quickly back and forth over the sprayed cookie sheet, leaving long, thin strands of sugar behind. Repeat this process, as often as needed, until you have a generous pile of spun sugar.

19. Gently gather the strands and wrap them around the croquembouche like a sugary gar-land. Add as little or as much spun sugar as you like. Serve immediately and encourage your guests to tear into the croque with reckless abandon.

20. Leftovers can be refrigerated in an airtight container for up to 3 days, but keep in mind that the humidity in the fridge will cause both the caramel and choux pastry to soften.

It's time to get crafty. Run out and grab a large piece of poster board and Scotch tape to help build your tower of cream puff power.

GINGERBREAD HOUSE
Makes one glorious gingerbread house

Sure, you can buy a gingerbread house kit for like five dollars literally everywhere during the holiday season. Sure, no one is actually going to eat it since it's going to sit out for a month and a half. Will that stop you? No. Take the phone off the hook, turn off the push notifications, and let's make a gingerbread house from scratch.

GINGERBREAD

2 sticks (8 ounces) unsalted butter, at room temperature

1 cup granulated sugar

1 cup molasses

1 teaspoon kosher salt

1 teaspoon baking soda

1 teaspoon ground cinnamon

1 teaspoon ground ginger

5 cups all-purpose flour

4 tablespoons water (if needed)

ROYAL ICING

1 bag (2 pounds) powdered sugar (7½ cups)

¾ cup meringue powder

Pinch of kosher salt

¾ cup water

1 teaspoon pure vanilla extract

DECORATION

Green gel food coloring

Sprinkle pearls

White sanding sugar

1. Make the gingerbread: In a stand mixer fitted with the paddle (or in a large bowl if using an electric hand mixer), beat the butter, granulated sugar, molasses, salt, baking soda, cinnamon, and ginger on medium-high speed, stopping to scrape down the sides of the bowl with a rubber spatula to make sure there are no butter lumps, until fluffy and lighter in color, 3 to 5 minutes.

2. With the mixer on low, slowly add the flour, 1 cup at a time, occasionally stopping to scrape down the sides of the bowl. Add just enough of the water to bring the dough together and mix until combined.

3. Divide the dough into four portions. Roll each portion to ¼ inch thick between sheets of parchment paper. Stack the sheets of dough on a baking sheet and chill for 30 minutes, or up to overnight, before cutting and baking.

4. Position two oven racks in the top and bottom thirds of the oven and heat the oven to 350°F. Line two rimmed baking sheets with parchment paper or silicone baking mats.

5. Use the templates on pages 195–197 to cut the walls and roof of your house from the sheets of dough. Set a template on the dough and trace along the edges with the tip of a sharp knife. Wipe the tip as needed to prevent the dough from dragging. Clear away the dough around the cut panel instead of trying to lift the cut piece up off the paper to prevent warping the shape. Slide the paper and cut piece of dough onto a baking sheet. Gather up the dough scraps and reroll as needed.

6. Baking times will vary depending on which component of the house you're working on. Larger pieces will take 10 to 15 minutes, while smaller ones could bake in under 10. The pieces are done when the dough has lost its raw sheen and the edges just begin to brown.

7. Allow the pieces to cool completely on the baking sheets before moving.

8. Repeat the rolling and cutting process to make trees and creatures to live around your house. Use cutters or freehand your designs. Roll tiny balls of dough between your fingertips to create pebbles for a walkway. Cut a 1½ x 1-inch rectangle for the door. Score lines down the front of the door before baking to make it look like wood planks. Stay close to the oven when baking smaller items, like the pebbles and door, because they will bake fast.

9. Make the royal icing: In a stand mixer fitted with the paddle (or in a large bowl if using an electric hand mixer), mix the powdered sugar, meringue powder, and salt on low speed until combined. Add the water and vanilla and mix on medium-low speed for about 5 minutes, until the icing is thick and bright white. Use immediately. Always keep the icing covered when not in use, because it dries out fast. Store in an airtight container, with plastic wrap pressed against the surface of the icing before adding the lid, in the fridge for up to 1 week.

10. As for the design of your gingerbread house, that is really up to you! To create ornate panels, pipe the designs on before you assemble the house, and allow the panels to dry out at room temperature overnight before building the house. Don't worry if any smudges or smears happen along the way. They can all be covered with icing "snow" in the end. Like Bob Ross said, "We don't make mistakes, just happy little accidents."

11. To make the roof panels: Fill a piping bag fitted with a small round tip with royal icing. Pipe a line of small arches along one of the long sides of a roof panel. Repeat until the panel is covered. To pipe the drops, hold the piping bag directly over the surface of the cookie, applying pressure to the bag to pipe a small dot. Release pressure and pull the bag away in the direction you want the drop to fall. Repeat three times over where each arch meets. Repeat the entire process on the other roof panel.

12. To make the wreaths and garlands: Tint 1 cup of royal icing green with gel food coloring. Add it to a piping bag fitted with a small leaf tip. Position the tip where you want to pipe a leaf so that the opening looks like a small open mouth. Apply pressure to the bag until the icing makes contact with the cookie, then release pressure and pull the bag up and away, leaving behind a little peak. Repeat as needed to fill in the wreath and garlands. Carefully add sprinkle pearl "ornaments" to the wet icing before it hardens.

13. To pipe the happy little trees: Pipe a scalloped line of frosting across the tree. Dampen the bristles of a small paintbrush and brush the frosting up toward the top of the tree. Repeat as needed.

14. Assemble the house: Decide where you want your happy little house to live. If it's staying with you, you can assemble it directly onto a platter or cutting board. If you'll be gifting the house, assemble on a wrapped cardboard cake drum. Examine the edges of each of the panels that make up the house and sand down any bumps or wonky bits with a brand-new nail file or microplane. Pipe a line of icing onto your cutting board or platter where you'd like the front of the house to stand. Press the cookie

into the icing and prop up with soup cans on either side. Do the same with the side panels, piping a line of frosting where the front and side panels meet. Add the back panel, piping a line on the plate. Then pipe icing into the vertical seams where the wall panels meet. Allow the icing to set for at least 4 hours, or up to overnight, before adding the roof.

15. Remove the cans from around the house and pipe lines of frosting up the roof peaks (the slanted portions) of the two side panels and across the top edge of the front panel. Set the front roof panel into place and slide a soup can in front to prop it up. Repeat with the back roof panel, then pipe a line of icing at the peak along the seam where the two roof panels meet. Prop up the back panel with another can. Allow the icing to set for at least 4 hours, up to overnight.

16. Fill in the scene around the house with the happy little trees, friendly creatures, gingerbread pebbles, and sanding sugar snow. You can do anything you want. This is your world.

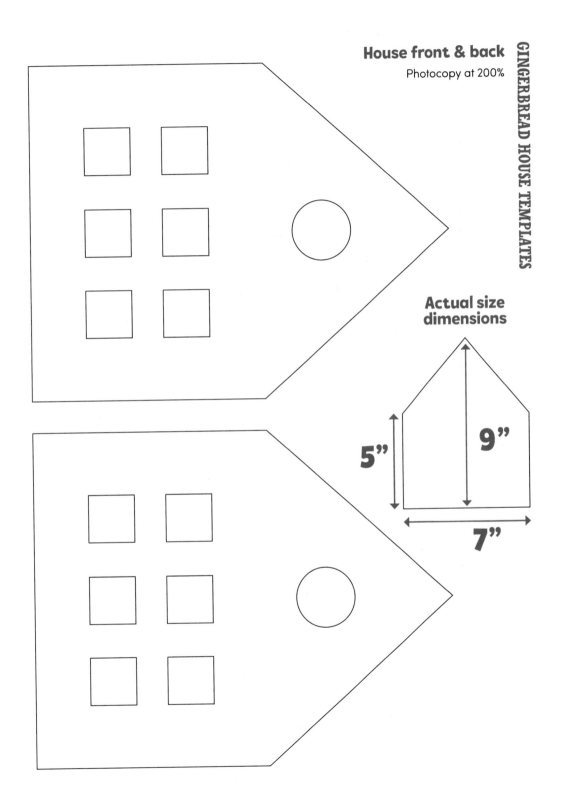

House front & back
Photocopy at 200%

GINGERBREAD HOUSE TEMPLATES

Actual size dimensions

5"

9"

7"

House sides: 7" x 5"

Photocopy two at 100%

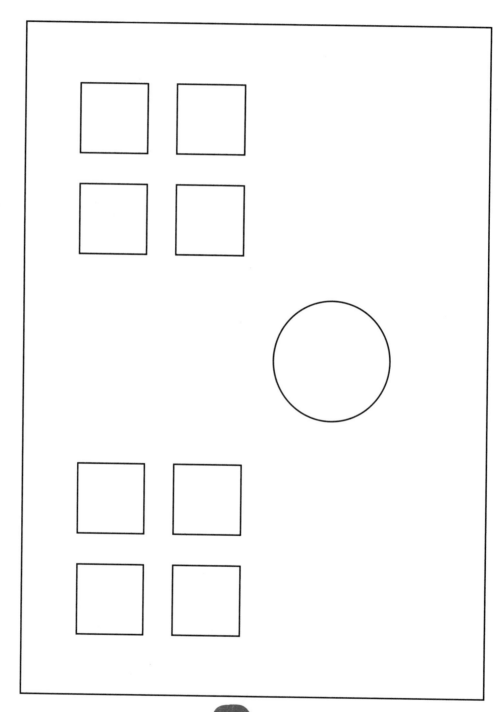

Roof panels: 8" x 5½"
Photocopy two at 100%

Reindeer & tree
Photocopy at 100%

ACKNOWLEDGMENTS

THE THANKS MUST BEGIN with my literary agent, Alison Fargis. Alison, this book would not have even been imagined without you. I wish everyone in the world would get to experience someone as intelligent and tenacious as you going to bat for them when there's every logical reason not to.

To my editor, Sarah Pelz, thank you for believing in this book, for your careful guidance throughout the process, and for being a joy to work with!

Julia Moskin, thanks for sliding into my DMs! I mean, maybe next time let's work on something that highlights one of my finer attributes in the *Times*? But this was a fantastic start! Thank you for including my weirdness in your article.

To all of the marketing and sales folks at Atria, thank you for all of your hard work and dedication while working on this book! And thank you in advance for selling lots of them!

To the book designer and illustrator who worked their magic on the cover and pages of this book, thank you for so beautifully bringing my bad habits to life!

To the editors who painstakingly sifted through every typo, misspelling, and poor grammar choice, thank you for making it look like I don't have more bad habits than I already do!

To Stacey Cramp and Vanessa Seder, thank you for your patience, persistence, and positive outlook while creating the beautiful images in this book. Everything is awesome!

To my family, both immediate and extended, thank you for imbuing sarcasm and irreverence in my DNA. I hail from a long and distinguished line of smart-asses, and for that I am eternally grateful.

To my patient and loving husband, Michael, thank you for managing life while I completed the manuscript and taking care of me with sushi and champagne. All of my hearts.

To my children, Maxwell and Violet, watching you grow into kind, intelligent, and unique people is the greatest source of inspiration I could ever ask for. Thanks for not burning the house down while Mommy worked on the computer. I love you both the most.

To my dad, thank you for loving food, writing, and me. To my mom, thank you for suggesting early on that I not take any shit from anybody. To my sister, thank you for helping me build the bakery, because without that and you, I don't know that any of this would have happened.

To everyone who's visited *Erin Bakes,* made one of my recipes, created a cake based on one of my tutorials, taken a class online or with me in person, you've taught me more than I could have ever taught you. I appreciate you all so much! **THANK YOU!**

METRIC CONVERSION CHART

PAN SIZE:

6 inches	15 cm
8 inches	20 cm
9 inches	23 cm
10 inches	25 cm
11 inches	28 cm
12 inches	30 cm
13 inches	33 cm
16 inches	40 cm
18 inches	45 cm

TEMPERATURE: GAS MARK:

250°F	120°C	½
300°F	150°C	2
325°F	165°C	3
350°F	180°C	4
375°F	190°C	5
400°F	205°C	6
425°F	220°C	7
450°F	230°C	8

VOLUME:

1 teaspoon	5 ml
1 tablespoon	15 ml
1 ounce	30 ml
¼ cup	60 ml
⅓ cup	80 ml
½ cup	120 ml
⅔ cup	160 ml
¾ cup	180 ml
1 cup	240 ml

WEiGHT:

¼ ounce	7 g
½ ounce	14 g
1 ounce	29 g
1½ ounces	43 g
2 ounces	57 g
4 ounces	113 g
8 ounces	227 g
1 pound	454 g
2 pounds	904 g

LENGTH:

⅛ inch	3 mm
¼ inch	6 mm
½ inch	12 mm
1 inch	2.5 cm

Metric Conversion Chart

INDEX

ABOUT THE AUTHOR

ERIN GARDNER is an award-winning cake designer, experienced pastry chef, author, blogger, and notorious procrastinator. She tries to not be late for most things, but she usually is. Little in the world brings her more joy than to feed people and make them happy.

Erin was named one of the top pastry pros in the country by *Martha Stewart Living.* Her work has also appeared in Oprah.com, the *New York Times, Town & Country, OK!* magazine, *Food Network Magazine, Brides,* and many other national and local publications. She's a regular contributor for *The Cake Blog* and *American Cake Decorating* magazine, frequent instructor at Stonewall Kitchen Cooking School, author of *Erin Bakes Cake,* and creator of ErinBakes.com.

The little big things that bring her the most joy are her love muffin children, stud muffin husband, and asthmatic cat, Lemon.